CHANGE
MASTERS

CHANGE MASTERS

HOW TO ACTUALLY MAKE THE CHANGES
YOU ALREADY KNOW YOU NEED TO MAKE

BARRY J. MOLTZ

VICARA
BOOKS

WASHINGTON, D.C.

Published in the United States by Vicara Books.

Vicara Books | www.vicarabooks.com

Cover Design: Faceout Studios
Interior Design: Jessica Angerstein

Cataloging-in-Publication Data is on file with the Library of Congress.

ISBN: 978-1-64687-062-2

Special Sales
Vicara Books are available at a special discount for bulk purchases for sales promotions and premiums, or for use in corporate training programs. Special editions, including personalized covers, a custom foreword, corporate imprints, and bonus content are also available.

Dedication

To my parents, Carole and Alan, may they rest in peace,
who taught me to act when I wanted to make a change and
not just complain about it.

As my dad always said:

"If a job is once begun

Do not leave it until it's done

Be it big or be it small, do it right or not at all."

"The only constant is change."
—HERACLITUS, ancient Greek philosopher (500 BC)

"Change isn't good or bad. It simply is."
—DON DRAPER, a character on the TV show, *Mad Men* (2007)

"Let go of the paddle. All the good stuff is downstream."
—As told to me by NICHOLE RAIRIGH,
CEO of The Apparel Agency (2020)

CONTENTS

ACKNOWLEDGMENTS

THIS IS MY seventh book and the easiest one to write so far. It is because I am so passionate about the topic and personally. I have struggled with change throughout my business and personal life. And I've seen so many small business owners also battle change even when they know it's the only thing to do.

I have always believed that talking about change is not enough. Taking action (almost any action will work) is critical for us to make progress in our businesses and our lives. Any action moves you forward from where you are right now—which is the fundamental start of any change.

This became especially important during the COVID-19 pandemic of 2020-2021 when a lot of the writing and research for this book took place while many of us were sheltering in place. Our normal lives were disrupted. Most companies and people were forced to reimagine their businesses and lives in real-time. These extreme circumstances pushed people to make changes and do things they never thought were possible. For example, I learned yoga from my wife, Sara. I planted an indoor garden. I biked inside on a trainer. I took Karate lessons and trained for my third-degree black belt test over Zoom. Sara and I cooked (and drank wine) a lot more. We bought takeout from restaurants in Chicago where we previously could never get a reservation. We eventually built our dream house in Scottsdale and waited out the pandemic there.

As you will learn in this book, not having a choice is one reason change happens, but it does not guarantee you won't go back to your old ways when the crisis recedes.

For this book, I want to thank Maria Anton, who collected and helped summarize much of the primary research around change. I also want to thank Rieva Lesonsky, my mentor and friend who edited this book, so you can understand what I was trying to say!

Finally, I am still hoping that my wife, Sara, will make a change and read one of my books!

Barry J. Moltz

Chicago, IL + Scottsdale, AZ

2020–2021

INTRODUCTION
WHY THIS BOOK

M Y WORK WITH thousands of small business owners over the past 20 years inspired me to write this new book. Well, that is not exactly true. More accurately, my frustration and the resulting challenges working with small business owners forced me to write this book. Let me explain.

I'm often asked by many companies and small business owners I don't know to help them. They are referred to me, hear me speak at an event, or find me online. Typically, they're feeling stuck by a problem, and their companies can't move forward. For example, their business growth is stagnant or worse—they're either losing money or not making enough to grow their companies or be motivated to keep going. After analyzing the situation, if I agree to work with them, we mutually decide on a go-forward strategy. I help them assemble a detailed plan to make any changes and the critical success factors and actions that need to be completed. They agree that taking these specific steps will help them solve their issues, grow their companies, and make more money.

And then, almost nothing happens.

Unfortunately, most small business owners implement a few easy steps but never take the critical or difficult ones that could make a difference. This has long frustrated me since we worked hard to develop a well-thought-out plan and were both excited to see the result. While it may not work perfectly once it is put into action, I know the plan will move their companies forward from where they are stuck now. I also feel bad because they are paying me their hard-earned cash to help them, and we both had agreed on the actions they needed to take and the time frame they needed to do it in. In the past, I tended to blame the inaction on myself. Did they not trust me enough to take significant steps, or did I just give them bad advice? However, after doing the research for this book, I realize I was not the main reason for their inability to change.

I wrote this book to figure out why small business owners do not make the changes or take the actions that they know will help them reach their goals. Where is the gap between the sincere intent to make these changes and the actions to actually do it? What holds most people back and keeps them stuck on the same path over and over again? Why are they still so comfortable not making any changes and staying on the path that clearly does not work for them—one that is not adding to their happiness or feeling of success? What steps do they need to take to slowly break free and start to make those changes today that will help them in the long run?

In this book, I reveal much of the psychological research around why change is so hard for so many people and the real-life strategies that every small business owner can employ to make the changes they need to make in their companies right now.

I am not trying to convince you to make a change but rather help you make the changes you already know you need to make but have not been able to do.

Later in the book, each solution section includes the exact steps you need to take to make a change in a particular area:

- **What You Do Now:** It's critical to identify what you are currently doing before implementing any change. While articulating this may be uncomfortable, it is a necessary step.

- **Where to Start to Make a Change:** Starting is the hardest part. Change needs to have a single-entry point to be effective.

- **How to Analyze:** You need to reflect on what is going on to see if you can make progress.

- **The First Steps:** It is critical to start small.

- **Why You Won't Do It Initially:** Despite all the preparation, some factors will still hold you back.

- **Take These Next Steps Instead:** Here are the easy steps to take to get a quick win.

- **How to Measure Successful Change:** How to tell if you are actually making progress and that change is being implemented.

These sections focus on how to make changes in the specific areas of sales and marketing, customer experience, money management, productivity, and your personal life.

In addition, in Chapter 5 and the appendix, there is a "Change Worksheet" that takes you through a 20-step process on how to execute successful change. Additional free copies of this worksheet can be found at www.changemastersbook.com

While the odds are stacked against you, as a small business owner, you have been here before. Being stuck and not changing is not inevitable. Instead, you can take steps to make the changes you need right now and become the ChangeMaster your company needs to thrive.

Change On!

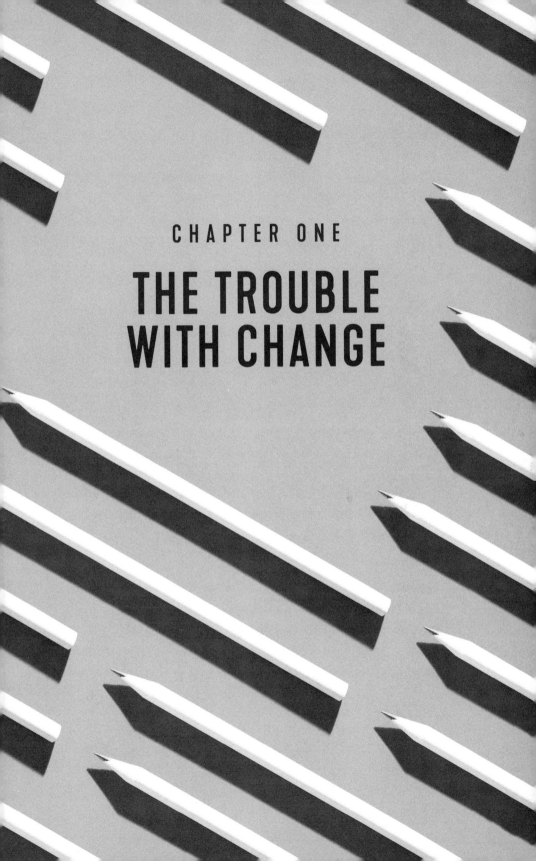

CHAPTER ONE

THE TROUBLE WITH CHANGE

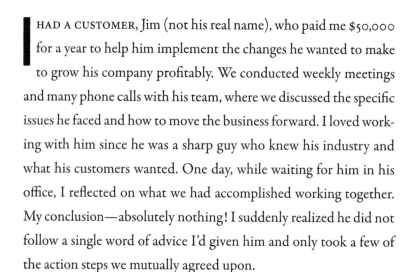

HAD A CUSTOMER, Jim (not his real name), who paid me $50,000 for a year to help him implement the changes he wanted to make to grow his company profitably. We conducted weekly meetings and many phone calls with his team, where we discussed the specific issues he faced and how to move the business forward. I loved working with him since he was a sharp guy who knew his industry and what his customers wanted. One day, while waiting for him in his office, I reflected on what we had accomplished working together. My conclusion—absolutely nothing! I suddenly realized he did not follow a single word of advice I'd given him and only took a few of the action steps we mutually agreed upon.

Every time we'd meet, Jim enthusiastically agreed that things needed to change. However, when it was time to act and follow the new, agreed-upon path, he hesitated. He stalled. He made excuses. He ultimately blamed me. This confused me because he strongly supported the need for change, yet he could barely get past the first step. I wondered why he'd initially hired me to help enact changes.

None of this made sense. Jim was an intelligent and logical entrepreneur who ran a somewhat successful company. He earned enough to support his family and their lifestyle and was smart enough to know his company was stuck and it needed to improve to get to the next level. Jim even realized he needed outside support from someone like me to make change happen. Plus, he was aware of his strengths and weaknesses as a leader and manager of his business.

And still—nothing actually changed. I later learned I wasn't alone in my experience. Jim frequently sought highly paid advice from sources like me but rarely followed any of it.

Why this sounds so familiar

Unfortunately, over the past 20 years working with small business owners, I've met too many Jims. It puzzled me why people would pay for expensive advice but use so little of it.

As I said in the Introduction, these experiences drove me to search for the answers. And I've uncovered several reasons why the struggle with change is so common:

 # People try to "buy" change.

I sell inexpensive online video courses to small business owners who don't have the resources to hire me personally or want to learn more after they've attended one of my events. Unfortunately, after selling many of these courses, I realized that 90% of the people who bought the system never started the first module!

I'm not saying they never completed the course. We all start things we never finish. I mean, they never even signed in to start one class even after paying for it. And they didn't ask for their money back. When I first noticed this, it shocked me. Why would anyone pay for a class and not start it? And if they never used it, why wouldn't they ask for their money back—especially when I offer a lifetime "no questions asked" money-back guarantee?

After talking to many of these non-users, I realized they thought buying the course was the equivalent of taking the key action to make the change. As a result, in their mind, no further action was required on their part. In other words, by purchasing the course, they thought they'd started to make the change. And if they still can't change, they can say that the course "did not work" for them!

In other cases, after they purchased the class, their desire to change faded, and they did not want to admit their lack of effort to themselves and were embarrassed to ask for a refund since they never started the course.

As silly as this seems, it happens more often than you'd think—especially with small business owners. Even in my consulting practice, customers think just by paying to work with me, they are making a change. These business owners seem to be satisfied paying to work toward change instead of taking the difficult steps actually to change. Unfortunately, this is a very expensive way never to change.

Working with me is their "proof" they tried to change, but it did not work. Their excuse: "I wanted to change. I hired a small business expert to help me, but even he couldn't get the company to change."

While this is not reality, it helps them stay in their comfort zone. They convince themselves that "it is better to have tried and failed than not to have tried at all." They then retreat to the comfort of doing the same old same old—even though it's not really working for them.

People don't want to do "more work" even if it results in positive change.

Intellectually, these small business owners know their companies need to change, but they are stuck. Doing the same things, the same ways, has produced enough success enabling them to keep going without making the drastic changes they'd need to get more than the same mediocre results. They may be stuck in a rut, but they're actually comfortable there. And it doesn't take any extra effort to remain—it's become easy and routine for them. Plus, they're not experiencing severe financial distress, so nothing forces them to put in the additional work to get on a different path.

Change is hard by itself, and altering long-practiced habits is even more challenging. But, given a choice, people will stick to the path they're currently on; it's just easier that way. Remember Newton's First Law of Motion: "An object at rest stays at rest, and an object in motion stays in motion with the same speed and in the same direction unless acted upon by an unbalanced force." I come into their companies as that unbalancing force, but ultimately when I leave, business owners stay where they were, headed in the same direction they were going before.

3 They are not in enough pain.

People only change when they are in so much physical, emotional, or financial pain that changing outweighs the fear of the unknown that change may bring. I have long believed people only buy a new product or service when they are in pain. Remember, consumers will always pay more for painkillers than vitamins.

The COVID-19 pandemic of 2020 forced many of us to pivot in a direction we never thought we'd take, but we had no choice when life as we knew it collapsed. In March of 2020, as the fear of the virus ramped up, supermarket shelves were empty, and we would eat whatever we could buy. For me, fear of eating unknown or unappetizing foods was better than going hungry.

These owners do not heed my advice because things in their companies are faring well enough that they can afford to keep doing it the way they have always done it. Not making a change will not drastically reduce their income or put them out of business. They are comfortable enough where they are without doing anything different.

They fear any change, especially the unknown.

Regardless of the future, these owners are comfortable continuing along the same path. They fear change will make business more difficult for them going forward. Although their companies are far from perfect, the status quo is always an easier path to travel. Remember the idiom; "Better the devil you know than the devil you don't"? In other words, even if you're stuck, you're better off sticking with the familiar than changing and plunging into the unknown—into what may be a disaster. Current comfort is always king.

As I've grown older, I have experienced this in my own life. The list of things I simply will not do grows bigger. I tell myself my body no longer allows me to do that. A great example is my karate practice over the last 20 years. As I've advanced through the black belt ranks, the curriculum got more difficult. This included doing more sweeps, falls, sparring and rolls. While I was never good at this to begin with, as I aged, I stopped doing these parts or pretended to do them. I reasoned it was no longer "safe" for me. Finally, my teacher, Jun Shihan Nancy, told me practicing karate this way was unacceptable. She understood that while these moves might be physically challenging, doing something was better than doing nothing. She told me that you must practice an accommodation that at least mimics the move that is safe for you. Doing something breaks the habit of doing nothing and forces change.

In fact, many small business owners who start as innovators stop taking risks because they fear change. For example, I sold my last large company in 1999 during the internet bubble. This was after I failed in my first two ventures, where I went out of business in one and was kicked out of the other by my partners.

After the sale, I didn't start another full-blown operational business because, having gone through so many ups and downs in the 1990s, I was afraid to take another big risk. Selling allowed me to pay the bank the $1.3M I owed them, build a healthy nest egg to pay for my children's college tuition, plus much more. So, I just was not willing to take another large-scale risk. While I have been fortunate to have done well financially over the past 20 years, I could not hit another small business" grand slam" because I feared losing what I had gained. While I am not always satisfied with the choices I've made, I realize my financial upside was limited without venturing into the unknown.

Many small business owners experience the same fear. They start out as innovators, but once they achieve success, they stop. They go into "protect mode" and focus on avoiding failure. They play not to lose instead of to win. You often see this in sports when teams with a big lead eventually lose the game because they play "not to lose".

Similarly, in business, so many innovations come from startup companies outside the industry. Why couldn't the taxi industry develop the Uber or Lyft application? Why didn't Blockbuster sell DVDs by mail or stream rentals like Netflix? The simple answer is they were making so much money in their current model there was no incentive to invest in a new one. While established businesses may risk their current revenue if they revolutionized their business models, upstart companies had nothing to lose, so they pursue change uninhibited.

5 They expect control.

Most small business owners seek control. This was one of the reasons they became business owners in the first place. Many people become entrepreneurs because they want to escape a controlling boss or system. Now, running their own companies, anything that threatens that control or status quo becomes the enemy.

Change is one of those things; it brings uncertainty and a loss of control over their future. These owners fear both.

They enjoy having what seems like complete control over their businesses and surrounding environment, even if it is not headed in the optimal direction. And even though they hire me, and I have the experience to help, they consider me an outsider, saying, "You don't know the business like I do." This becomes their excuse for not making changes. Or they get tired of someone like me pushing them to change because they'd have to admit what they're doing is not working, and they fear losing control if they did something different.

6 DIY: They trust solely in themselves.

Often, small business owners like to do it themselves. They trust their own abilities to get things done and always have difficulty delegating significant responsibilities to others. Most small businesses do not operate as a traditional hierarchical organization where decision-making is distributed by level or area of responsibility. Instead, they work in a hub-and-spoke manner where every decision comes inefficiently to the owner at the center of the organizational circle.

Small business owners value their own opinions above all others. This is not a negative, but a characteristic of founders who inherently believe they are right and everyone else is wrong. This confidence, misplaced as it is, enables them to undertake the risks of starting up.

When they started, they trusted their instincts, and it brought them enough success to be comfortable. So, when it comes down to it, why should they change? Are they "that wrong"? Isn't their way really the "correct" way? This kind of thinking has helped them until now, so why change or act on another point of view?

But if we are to grow our companies, we must constantly change with the market. COVID-19 showed all of us that reimagining our businesses was required to adapt to the market. Going forward, the changes you should make may not be as drastic as what you had to do during the pandemic of 2020, but the need to change and evolve is always there. In fact, 2,500 years ago, Heraclitus, a Greek philosopher, said, "Change is the only constant in life."

Yes, despite knowing all of this, you continue to resist.

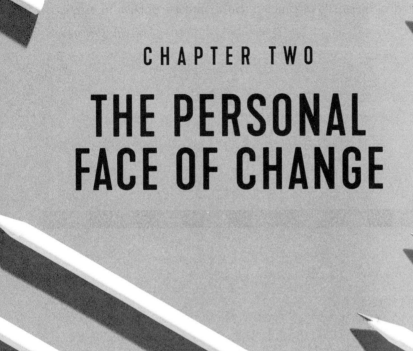

CHAPTER TWO

THE PERSONAL
FACE OF CHANGE

UNDERSTAND THE CHALLENGE of change because it has always been hard for me. I like routine. I can go for years eating the same thing for breakfast. Currently, that's two waffles and an English muffin. When I travel, it's typically eggs, potatoes, and fruit at the hotel. I always sleep on the same side of the bed, whether I'm home or staying at a hotel without Sara. I like sitting in the same seat at the dinner table and in the same place when I watch television at night. In fact, it bothers me if Sara is sitting in "my" space.

Yes, like many people, I am a creature of habit. But for me, it's more than that. Habit is part of my balance of life. Before the pandemic (and hopefully after), from week to week, I never really know what city I will be in, who I will be working for, or what audience I'll be speaking to. I tell myself these habits give me the stability and balance in my personal life that I'm missing in the inherently unstable career I've chosen as an entrepreneur.

I'm not totally intractable, and over the years, I have changed—but it's been difficult. I did not make most of these changes voluntarily. Events, people, and intense internal motivations forced my hand when it seemed I had no choice. Here are some personal examples.

Big corporate employee to small business entrepreneur

In 1990, I left the comforts of IBM to pursue a new business adventure working at a small company as director of sales. After nine years at IBM, I was getting the entrepreneurial itch to go out on my own. I read *Growing a Business* by Paul Hawken, which showed me the idyllic path to creating a company and a culture of my own away from a big corporation. It made me want to give up all the corporate traditions and trappings at IBM, like wearing blue suits and instead, wear jeans to work!

At the same time, my client, Bob Bernard, the CEO at Whittman-Hart, offered me an opportunity to join his company as director of sales. I hesitated, but I disliked my boss, George (yes, his real name), because he had an outsized ego. I assumed "a real business" would not put such mediocre people in positions of power. (Another illusion that would burst many times over.) In fact, George used to hold sales contests where the first prize was lunch with him. (I always mused what would be the second prize—two lunches with him?). In addition, I was already experimenting with the idea of business ownership through a side hustle called "Yes We Deliver" (think of it as a forerunner to Grubhub). It was a physical handbook of places that delivered in Chicago that I produced with my best friend, Zane, his wife, Joan, and my future spouse, Sara. Finally, I didn't want to deal with George anymore, and I quit IBM. Unfortunately, I only realized later how ill-prepared I was for that business change.

At IBM, there was a famous brand behind every call I made and every proposal I sent. At my new company, I had a small sales team with little training and only a local reputation. I was also unprepared for the "cutthroat cage match" atmosphere embedded at Whittman-Hart. Everyone tried to curry favor with the CEO by stabbing others in the back. By comparison, it was all so civil at IBM. Mercifully, I was fired a year after I arrived by Bob, who had hired me.

I don't look back on this as a negative experience. I knew my future was not working at IBM but instead running my own business. Working at a small business like Whittman-Hart, even for only a year, was the path I had to follow to learn how to start my own company. After leaving IBM, getting fired from Whittman-Hart, going out of business in my first company, I was then fired from my second startup by my partners, who I had met through a classified ad at *The Chicago Tribune*. You can find many great things to buy in the classified section of a newspaper but not partners. They eventually pushed me out to bring in a new shareholder with deeper pockets. (A year later, they went out of business.)

These changes were very painful. But in hindsight, I see them as necessary, and they transformed me into the type of businessperson I am today. Failure is a valuable lesson. These failures made me realize to become a successful business owner, I would need to change. For example, one of the reasons my first business (It was called "Yes We Deliver") failed was I didn't have enough money to attract the best people. And I didn't think I needed to. I had always thought you could hire random part-or full- time employees to fit any role as long as you gave them a process, a great product, and the right tools. I was wrong. And I learned I needed to have enough money to hire people who could execute the plan effectively.

In my second business, after being thrown out by my partners after a year, I realized having a good idea is not enough to build a successful business around. You need to surround yourself with like-minded people that you can trust.

So, when I started my third business, I focused on what type of person my partner was and made sure I could trust him. He happened to be the husband of a woman I went to college with. That business was ultimately successful, and we sold it during the internet bubble of 1999.

Non-athlete to second-degree karate black belt

I am not a flexible person physically or emotionally, even though I've taken karate for almost 20 years. And although I am a third-degree black belt now, I'm likely one of the least skilled people at my rank at my school. But I keep going because I enjoy the community, the self-defense skills it teaches me, the memorization it requires, and the physical activity it requires at each class.

But when asked to learn a new difficult technique, my immediate reaction is to say I'll never be able to do that. I know it's the fear of being hurt or injured while performing that holds me back. It froze me so much that there were periods where I would simply stop training. Sometimes I would arrive at the school, not go in and turn around and go home. Over the years, even though I've learned I can adapt to do part of the move, my inclination is still to say "no" when taught something new. In my mind, it's safer not to change.

But I have kept training. I have been hurt—experienced lots of broken ribs, toes, and pulled hamstrings. And it's been worth it. I remember when I tested for five hours for my first-degree black belt, my teacher, Jun Shihan Nancy, said to me, "Now you can call your-self an athlete."

During the pandemic, I trained to achieve my third-degree black belt in karate. In my style at this level, I need to know hundreds of different sequences ranging from 3 concurrent moves to patterns of 56 moves. Needless to say, it's a lot to remember and have your body execute each of the moves one at a time. But as I learn these movements, I remember the words of our "Grandmaster" Kaicho Tadashi Nakamura, "Technique rather than strength. Spirit rather than technique." The change I made over the years was breaking the vast amount of material down to the smallest elements and learning those first, instead of trying to learn too many things at one time. While this does not help me with perfect form, this method does allow me to keep learning and progressing toward bigger goals.

Bending and lifting

In 2003, I hurt my back badly. While on a trip to France with my family, my back started to spasm after riding a horse in the

Camargue. On that vacation, I was in bed, flat on my back for about five days. For the next 10 years, I was afraid to lift anything for fear of reinjuring my back. This prevented me from experiencing the joy of picking up my children when they were young. After a lot of physical therapy, where I learned how to lift correctly, I realized it was not a physical limitation. As with any change, the resistance to making progress was all in my mind. I was afraid I would get hurt again (although I no longer ride horses).

Learning from a professional physical therapist how to bend and lift again in a controlled environment gave me the confidence to do it in my everyday life. So, while I still battle the emotional demons whenever I have to lift something, the fear no longer stops me from doing it.

I was able to change because I realized not being able to lift my young children was a big problem, and I did not want to go through their early years not holding them. As a result, I found a professional who could help me with my problem and practiced the change repeatedly until I could deal with the fear.

Does this sound familiar to you? If it's any comfort (it was to me), the research says fearing change is not solely your fault. Instead, it's your brain's fault!

As Melissa Galt, Interior Design Business Coach, says, "Your brain is a pattern-making machine; when it comes to change, your brain is not your friend."

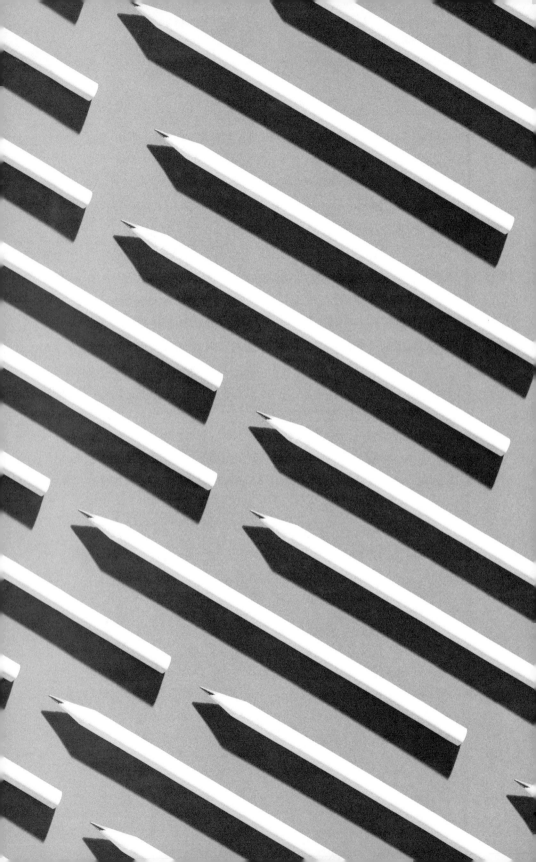

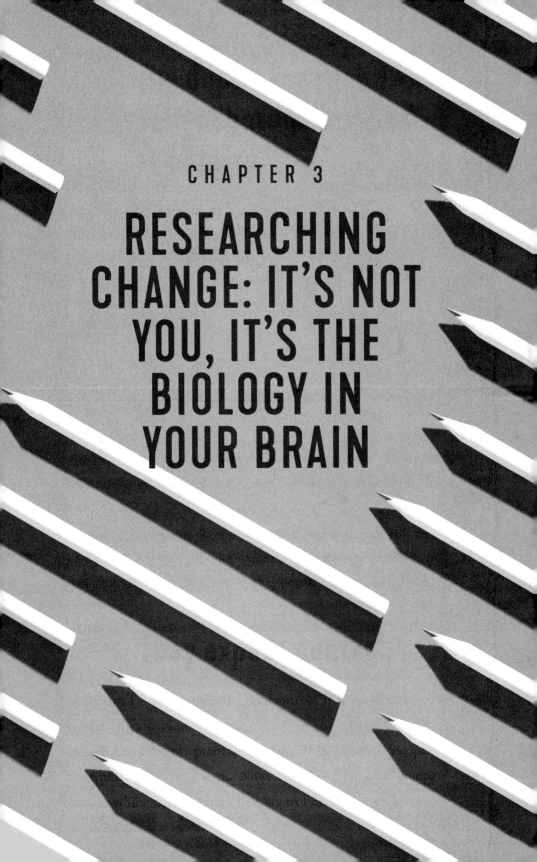

CHAPTER 3

RESEARCHING CHANGE: IT'S NOT YOU, IT'S THE BIOLOGY IN YOUR BRAIN

Note to readers: This chapter is about the science behind why change is hard. Therefore, it does get a little technical. If you are not interested in this, you can skip to Chapter 5 that shows you solutions to help you make the changes you want.

IT'S NOT YOUR fault you're resistant to change. For the survival of the human species, you are biologically programmed not to change over a short period of time. Therefore, any personal change means pain to your brain. Furthermore, making an organizational change, such as inside a small business, is unexpectedly difficult because it promotes discomfort for the entire team. Here is what is actually happening biologically and why:

It's the basal ganglia's fault.

There are neurological reasons why people are resistant to change; biologically, our brains are not wired for change. When you proactively set out to learn something new—ride a mountain bike, drive a car, or practice skiing—you tend to be very conscious of what you are doing. Your brain creates pathways that start out weak, but as you practice that activity repeatedly, over time, those connections get stronger, and it becomes a hardwired habit. You can ride or drive without having to consciously think about it. How often have you driven someplace, and after arriving, you don't remember driving there? Activities we do by rote are stored in the basal ganglia, the part of the brain that controls habits. They require less energy to execute and operate. Instinctively, we want to save energy whenever possible, so the body is free to do other essential things.

Think about your morning commute. You're driving a car on the same road every day. As a result, you no longer have to think about how to get there. However, one day you encounter a detour, and you must take a different route. Suddenly, you are forced to pay attention to what you're doing and change your hardwired driving habit. Unfortunately, making this type of change requires the brain to do more work, making us feel slightly uncomfortable.

Similarly, I have hiked a trail by our home in Arizona hundreds of times, up and down the mountain. One time, I decided to do the hike in reverse; in other words, I hiked up the trail I typically took down the mountain and hiked down the trail I usually took to climb up. I was surprised how much I had to pay attention to my footing during this hike, even though I was on the same trail I had so often hiked in the opposite direction. In addition, I noticed desert fauna this time that I had never seen when hiking in the other direction!

Our brain can also interpret any change as "wrong" and begin to fight against it. The brain can detect differences between expectation and what is happening. For example, if we expect that something should be cold, and then it's hot, the brain will emit intense error signals in the amygdala, the area of the brain that's responsible for fear. This experience is called an "amygdala hijack" or a sudden and overwhelming fear, as described by Daniel Goleman in *Emotional Intelligence*. In the same way, when you need to make a big change in your small business, your brain thinks something is wrong, and you feel stress and physical discomfort about making any new adjustment.

2 Our expectations shape our reality.

People's preconceptions of what will happen to them have a significant impact on what they eventually feel. For example, if people anticipate comfort, they will feel comfortable; if they expect pain, they will perceive pain. As David Rock, author of *Quiet Leadership,* and Jeffrey Schwartz, a research psychiatrist at the School of Medicine at the University of California at Los Angeles, say, "People experience what they expect to experience."

The assumptions we make about ourselves and our world are known as mental maps. We behave according to the mental maps we create. These mental maps, explains forensic psychologist Katherine Ramsland, are how we "mentally navigate our world" and help us make sense of what we see.

We are all born with billions of neurons in our brains. As our brain develops, our life experiences affect the way our neurons connect. The pathways of these connections "control our intellectual, emotional, psychological, physiological and physical responses to what we do every day," writes researcher JF Mustard. So, in the future, when faced with the opportunity to make a change, we instead avoid it.

How, then, is it possible to facilitate change? Rock and Jeffery write, "Large-scale behavior change requires a large-scale change in mental maps. This, in turn, requires some kind of event or experience that allows people to provoke themselves, in effect, to change their attitudes and expectations more quickly and dramatically than they normally would." And so, the COVID-19 lockdown across the United States in 2020 forced people to change their daily habits from working to shopping to socializing from in-person to primarily online.

3 The brain likes longevity and familiarity.

Many small business owners who contact me say they want to change because their current path is unsustainable. However, although people say they want to change, on a subconscious level their brains don't like uncertainty, prefer familiarity, and want to stay in precisely the same place no matter what is going on. So, for the brain, longer is better. The length of time something has been established inside the brain seems to indicate its overall benefit.

One study found this bias when evaluating various items, including European chocolate. Participants were asked to compare the same type of chocolate. They were told one sample came from a 73-year-old company, and the other was from a business that started selling three years ago. They preferred the chocolate from the older company. The researchers refer to the bias as a "non-rational heuristic"—an internal guideline we use to make decisions that don't always make sense. In this example, why would chocolate from a company that has been around longer really be better?

According to psychologist Heidi Grant-Halvorson, "It's not just that people fear change, though they undoubtedly do. It's that they genuinely believe (often on a subconscious level) that when you've been doing something a particular way for some time, it *must* be a good way to do things. And the *longer* you've been doing it that way, the better it is." Small business owners who have been successful for a while subconsciously want to keep doing what has brought them success and fear changing to a new path, despite what the evidence tells them.

Grant-Halvorson says, to overcome this bias, you first need to be aware the bias exists.

 # The devil speaks to you.

Most of us are familiar with the expression "the devil you know is better than the one you don't." In fact, many small business owners follow this precept when making decisions, particularly, for example, when replacing a poor-performing employee. As researchers Scott Eidelman and Christian S. Crandall wrote, "The principal rule of induction is that we expect the future to be like the past. [In other words] we effortlessly and unconsciously expect gravity to hold us to the ground every morning."

This fear of change is caused by uncertainty. As I noted previously, our brains rely on our habits, from how we shop for groceries to how we respond to criticism. Relying on repetition and the things we perceive as rules makes things easier for the brain, giving it less work to do. This means even if some of your habits are hurting you, your brain still resists changing them. A separate study by Eidelman and Crandall calls this "existence bias," a tendency for people to infer good from mere existence. When an object or event represented the status quo, the item was considered "good and desirable."

So how does this affect change? Basically, any alternatives to the status quo are immediately at a disadvantage. As Eidelman and Crandall note, "Because of a bias favoring mere existence, not only is it difficult to effect social change, but it can be difficult simply to persuade people to think favorably about alternatives." This is because your brain does not usually consider something new good for you.

 # The dopamine rush from self-sabotage instead of change.

Many small business owners would agree that sometimes we are our own worst enemies. Self-sabotage is the actions we take that get in the way of us achieving our goals. For example, a small business owner might:

- Keep an employee who consistently shows they can't (or won't) do their job. (The devil you know adage again.)

- Postpone meeting with their accountant, who can explain what is going on in their business so they can make smarter financial decisions. (Not knowing actual financial results is easier than knowing.)

- Not call a customer who owed them a lot of money (Afraid they will never pay and with it the fear of rejection).

- Not follow up on a potentially significant sales opportunity. (Again, afraid or rejection, and you will need to find a new prospect.)

Why do so many of us practice self-sabotage? It depends on the expert you ask. According to clinical and forensic neuropsychologist Judy Ho, "The propensity to commit self-sabotage is built into our neurobiology" and is what has allowed us as humans to evolve and survive as a species. We are programmed to strive for things that make us feel good. Every time we achieve a goal and feel good, we get a dopamine rush—and are incentivized to repeat the process all over again. It would seem like this is a good thing and push us to achieve our goals."

But our bodies also get that same dopamine rush when we try to avoid something threatening. Our brain tries to keep those two drives in equilibrium. However, if they get out of whack, and the desire to avoid a threat becomes greater than the desire to attain a goal, that's when self-sabotage crops up. Ho writes, "Self-sabotage occurs when your drive to reduce threats is higher than your drive to attain rewards."

Clinical psychologist Ellen Hendriksen cites several psychological reasons for self-sabotage: First, she states that some people feel worthless despite achievements. You don't feel like you deserve to be successful, or you may be afraid of succeeding. If you have achievements but also feel worthless, you experience cognitive dissonance—a conflict of feelings. To get rid of that feeling of dissonance, people will "pull the plug" on their successes because while "it feels bad to fail, but not as bad [as it does] to succeed." Next, many people like to "control their failure." As Hendrikson writes, "It feels better to control your own failure than to let it blindside you."

Many people also suffer from "imposter syndrome," thinking that if others perceive them as too successful, society may call them out as a fraud. Many small business owners experience imposter syndrome because they are not sure why they succeeded. Some even believe they don't deserve their success; despite the risks and hard work it took to achieve it. For example, when I sold my last business, even though I worked hard, I felt my success had more to do with luck and timing (during the internet bubble of 1999) than anything I did.

I have also seen failing to change as a handy scapegoat: If the change doesn't work out, then it is easy to blame yourself for the failure. Strangely, feeling sorry for ourselves is comforting.

Finally, some people don't like to be bored. Some of us actually enjoy the feeling of chaos and instability. Many successful small business owners are bored, so they stir things up to entertain themselves through self- sabotage. It also keeps them in control by throwing everyone else in the company off balance.

In Australia, this self-sabotage sometimes happens due to "Tall Poppy Syndrome." I wrote about it in my book, *Bounce: Failure, Resiliency and The Courage for Your Next Great Success.* When I visited his college in Tasmania, Professor Colin **Jones told** me, "In our country, people want to see you fail. Everyone wants to say, 'I told you so; I told you it was never going to work.' So, you have to find a way to insulate yourself from all the negativity. We have a thing—Tall Poppy Syndrome—which simply means people always try to bring down the high achievers." (The origin of the expression: When farmers grow poppies, they typically cut off the tops of those that are growing too fast in an attempt to maintain homogeneity.)

 Perfectionism is a change problem.

People like to be good at what they do. They are afraid to try something new because they fear they won't be immediately good at it, so they avoid making any changes in their lives. According to scholars like Dana Harari at the Georgia Institute of Technology, who wrote the research report "Is Perfect Good?", perfectionism is "striving for flawlessness, setting excessively high standards for performance, and evaluating one's behavior overcritically." It's a trait that researchers Thomas Curran and Andrew P. Hill say can be blamed on society. They write, "From the 1980s onward, neoliberal governance in the United States, Canada, and the United Kingdom has emphasized competitive individualism, and people have seemingly responded, in kind, by agitating to perfect themselves and their lifestyles." Their research shows perfectionism is currently a growing trait among college students.

When small business owners delay or choose not to make changes in their businesses, it could be because they are perfectionists, and are waiting for that perfect moment to act—when sales are booming, profits are up, the economy is strong, and they have the ideal team in place. All of this, of course, never comes, and neither does the self-promised change.

Researchers call this "excellence-seeking perfectionism." Patricia Di Bartolo, a professor of clinical psychology, says when people are worried about being perfect, they become paralyzed, missing deadlines because they're afraid they can't meet the standards they've set for themselves. "They engage," she says, "in this vicious cycle where nothing is ever good enough, so they never make any forward movement.".

A sales manager, Mark (not his real name) I used to work with at Whittman-Hart, warned against waiting to take the next step until you create the perfect "all singing and dancing" product or service.

Doing this, he said, actually delays taking the steps that could help us learn what the best course of action might be.

A second type of perfectionism can also be a problem. "Failure-avoiding perfectionism" is an obsessive concern with failing to reach specific standards. Researcher Brian Swider writes, "Failure-avoiding perfectionists are constantly worried their work is not quite right or good enough and believe they will lose respect from others if they do not achieve perfection." Jeff Szymanski, the executive director of the International OCD Foundation, calls it a "phobia of mistake making." He adds, "It is the feeling that, 'If I make a mistake, it will be catastrophic.'" These people cite others who aren't perfect as a reason why they need to stay perfect.

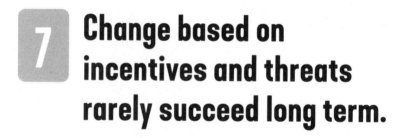

7 Change based on incentives and threats rarely succeed long term.

For years economic incentives have been considered sufficient to motivate change. So many small business owners naturally think offering increased financial rewards to their employees will be incentive enough to initiate change. This is especially notable since the owners themselves do not make any changes despite the incentive to earn more profits. According to an article published in the *Journal of Economic Perspectives*, "Economics often emphasize that 'incentives matter,'" and the "basic 'law of behavior' is that higher incentives will lead to more effort and higher performance."

However, as experts David Rock and Jeffrey Schwartz point out, "Behaviorism doesn't work. Change efforts based on incentive and threat (the carrot and the stick) rarely succeed—especially in the long run." In my experience, incentives can get people to change a particular behavior for the short term, but as soon as the motivation or threat goes away, they return to their old behavior patterns.

It's likely then that money isn't as strong a motivator as we think. Sociologist Philip Slater said, "The idea that everybody wants money is propaganda circulated by wealth addicts to make themselves feel better about their (own) addiction."

Financial incentives are often ineffective because while money can motivate someone to do something, it doesn't mean it will make a person *want* to do something to change. Human behavior expert Alfie Kohn writes, "The more you use rewards to "motivate" people, the more they tend to lose interest in whatever they had to do to get the rewards." Many people consider gaming the system to get a reward. None of this makes genuine change happen; it just gets you a temporary result.

A client of mine, Kevin (not his real name), had an accountant who was required to complete the bank reconciliations by the 15th of every month. He could not get this employee to finish the reconciliations on time, so one month he provided a $500 incentive to encourage him to complete it. Not surprisingly, the accountant met his deadline—that month. Of course, Kevin now expected to get the reconciliations by the 15th of every month. And of course, not surprisingly, the accountant never turned them in on time again without getting an incentive. In this case, the accountant temporarily changed to get $500 but never permanently altered his behavior. Incentives or threats may provide a short-term boost to the "gamers" who just want the money but never offer real change.

 # As you age, your brain gets lazy.

Young brains have a lot of flexibility which allows children to learn things quickly. But by the time we reach age 25, our brains have become so dependent on existing neural pathways and patterns, learning new things or a way to do something new becomes more difficult. For example, years ago, when my young son and I practiced karate together, he would learn the new moves more quickly than me. Tara Swart, a neuroscientist and author of *Neuroscience for Leadership*, describes an "older" brain as "inherently lazy" and says it will always "choose the most energy-efficient path."

As discussed, any time we learn a new habit, a new connection or neural pathway is formed in the brain. As we repeat that habit, we use that neural pathway over and over. The task will become a habit as our brain prefers to use that quick and efficient pathway.

"Human beings develop neural pathways. And the more we use those neural pathways over the years, they become very stuck and deeply embedded, moving into deeper portions of the brain," explains Deborah Ancona, Director of the MIT Leadership Center at the MIT Sloan School of Management. "By the time we get to the age of 25, we have so many existing pathways that our brain relies on, it's hard to break free of them."

Management experts today have realized through neuroplasticity (the ability of neural networks in the brain to change through growth and reorganization), they can help business leaders create change by rewiring the brain to forge new and stronger neural pathways through new patterns. "Over time, by raising awareness again and again of the 'autopilot' brain pathways that 'run' us by habit, we can recognize the barriers that are holding us back in our own minds and forge a path toward positive change," explains Tara Swart. "It's also crucial to replace the old thought habits with new, more consciously chosen, empowering ones. There is no way to 'unlearn' what you already know; instead, you need to habituate new ones."

Ancona and Swart teach an MIT Sloan Executive Education course called "Neuroscience for Leadership," which applies neurological research to leadership development.

According to Ancona, "In leadership education, we talk a lot about inertia and the inability to change. In my own work on sensemaking, the most difficult challenge for leaders is being stuck with seemingly fixed internal mental models."

Swart says, "What we know about neuroplasticity now is that, within limits, you can change yourself. You can learn to be a leader at all levels—as a self-authoring person, respected husband, role-model mother, successful entrepreneur, or CEO of an iconic brand."

Failure to track progress harms change.

According to the authors of a study on the Intention-Behavior Gap, "One reason goal pursuit can be derailed is because people fail to monitor their progress." Further, the authors say, "Keeping track of progress (e.g., using a diary) increases the likelihood that intentions are achieved, perhaps because monitoring progress serves to identify discrepancies between current and desired states, and maintains attention on the focal goal."

It would make sense then for people to monitor their progress to help them achieve goals. However, another study reports that "people have a tendency to 'bury their head in the sand' and intentionally avoid or reject information that would help them monitor their goal progress." This psychological phenomenon is known as the "ostrich problem." Put more simply, people are afraid to know about their own progress!

People avoid monitoring their progress because they don't want to chance not reaching their goals and experience the pain of disappointment. This is known as loss aversion, coined by psychologists Amos Tversky and Daniel Kahneman, where the pain of losing is twice as powerful as the pleasure of gaining. In other words, "people would rather accept a small but certain reward over the chance of at a larger gain."

According to researchers Nira Liberman and Reuven Dar, failure to monitor "may reduce one's focus on the goal and increase the likelihood of being sidetracked by irrelevant activities."

But what's also interesting is loss aversion works on a neural level. Researchers conducted a study on loss aversion and monitored brain activity. Russell A. Poldrack, a professor of psychology at Stanford University, says, "The brain regions that process value and reward may be silenced more when we evaluate a potential loss than they are activated when we assess a similar-sized gain."

10 Your intentions are not the same as your actions.

The gap between intentions, which are self-instructions to perform particular behaviors or obtain specific outcomes, and then acting on those intentions can be very large. According to research, our intentions get translated into actions only about half the time. So, what causes this gap, and is it possible to bridge it?

One reason for the gap is the way intentions and goals are framed from the start. To lessen the gap, goals framed in terms of promotion over prevention, autonomy over nonautonomy, and learning or mastery over performance are more likely to be attained in the long run.

Here are how the conflicts get framed in people's minds.

Promotion vs. prevention: According to social psychologist Heidi Grant Halvorson, "Promotion-focused goals are thought about in terms of achievement and accomplishment. They are about doing something you would *ideally* like to do...they are about maximizing *gains* (and avoiding missed opportunities)."

In contrast, "prevention-focused goals are thought about in terms of safety and danger. They are about fulfilling responsibilities—doing the things you feel you *ought* to do and minimizing *losses*—trying to hang on to what you've got."

Autonomy vs. nonautonomy: Autonomous goals (which reflect personal interests and values rather than something you feel compelled to do by external or internal pressures) are associated with greater goal progress over time than nonautonomous goals, writes Richard Koestner, a professor of psychology at McGill University. Researchers Edward L. Deci and Richard M. Ryan say people driven by autonomous motivation strongly identify internally with a goal. In contrast, people driven by controlled (nonautonomy) motivation will act in a certain way—either to obtain external rewards or avoid punishment.

Koestner's study, "Reaching One's Personal Goals: A Motivational Perspective Focused on Autonomy," found that "autonomous goal motivation can lead directly to greater goal progress by allowing individuals to exert more effort, experience less conflict, and feel a greater sense of readiness to change their behavior."

Learning or mastery vs. performance: Learning or mastering goals increase your competence; performance goals are about mastering competence. Stanford University psychologist Carol Dweck found that when there is an overemphasis on performance, "failure is more likely to provoke a helpless response" because of the additional pressure.

Learning goals, on the other hand, "showed a clear mastery-oriented pattern" and "in the face of failure," [subjects] did not worry about their intellect, they remained focused on the task, and they maintained their effective problem-solving strategies." Moreover, they weren't concerned about showing someone else how well they can do it.

What we want to do vs. what we are supposed to do: Another reason for the gap can be the conflict between what a person wants to do versus what they feel they should do. For example, a student writing a paper knows they need to continue working, but they also want to take a break. The "want," according to researchers Cat Taylor, Thomas L. Webb, and Paschal Sheeran, "can give rise to justifications for indulgence that can undermine the realization of intentions." During times of high stress, what we want or think we deserve can be over-prioritized.

Your brain's battle between short term satisfaction and long-term goals: The field of neuroeconomics, which investigates the mental and neural processes that drive economic decision-making, has found that "humans don't always work in the ways that economic theory would predict," explains Jonathan Cohen, co-director of the Princeton Neuroscience Institute at Princeton University. The Institute conducted a study that found two areas of the brain compete for control over behavior when a person attempts to balance near-term rewards with long-term goals. The study showed that decisions involving the possibility of immediate reward activated the parts of the brain influenced heavily by neural systems associated with emotion. In other words, when people got close to getting a reward, their emotional brain took over.

"Our emotional brain has a hard time imagining the future, even though our logical brain clearly sees the future consequences of our current actions," explains David Laibson, a professor of economics at Harvard University. "Our emotional brain wants to max out the credit card, order dessert, and smoke a cigarette. Our logical brain knows we should save for retirement, go for a jog, and quit smoking."

James Clear, the author of *Atomic Habits,* calls this "akrasia," when you do one thing even though you know you should do something else. He cites the example of author Victor Hugo who, while on deadline writing *The Hunchback of Notre Dame,* instead spent a year entertaining friends and doing other things to the dismay of his publisher.

The Princeton researchers concluded that impulsive choices for short-term rewards result from the emotion-related parts of the brain winning out over the abstract-winning parts, which supports the view that psychological factors other than pure reasoning often drive people's decisions.

The goal is too optimistic or too hard to achieve: Goals are easier to attain when tasks are easier to perform; over-optimistic goals are less likely to be fulfilled. But, according to researchers Paschal Sheeran and Thomas L. Webb, "goal difficulty is a function of the resources, ability, skills, cooperation, opportunities, and time and effort needed to realize the goal." However, Sheeran and Webb also say people will spend more time trying to achieve optimistic goals versus realistic ones.

CHAPTER 4

ONE SOLUTION IS TO USE SCIENCE TO TRAIN YOUR BRAIN FOR CHANGE

Note to readers: This chapter is about how science suggests you make changes, which can get technical. If you are not interested in this, you can skip to Chapter 5 that shows you solutions to help you make the changes you want.

A S DISCUSSED, PEOPLE only change when they are in tremendous pain. Even so, there are considerable barriers to stopping how we currently do things. As a result of its survival instinct, your brain resists change and fights you every step of the way—unless there is incredible danger.

So how can you help your brain make changes? Here are three starting principles:

1 Focus is power.

In *The Strangest Secret*, published in 1957, author Earl Nightingale noted how we are what we think about. Rhonda Byrne popularized this in *The Secret* 50 years later. In other words, repeated, purposeful, and focused attention can lead to long-lasting personal change. For example, if you are on the golf course and keep focusing on not hitting the ball into the sand trap—that's exactly where your ball will end up. In other words, the more you focus on something repeatedly (positive or negative), the more you are likely to achieve it. As you have always been told, practice does indeed make perfect.

You can grow new neuron pathways by focusing on the parts of the brain you use less frequently. New neurons will connect to the strong neurons already in your brain and build new pathways. For example, to stimulate your brain, you could learn a new language. According to neuroscientist Tara Swart, any activity requiring "conscious processing of inputs, conscious decision-making, complex problem solving, memorizing complex concepts, planning, strategizing, self-reflection, regulating our emotions and channeling energy from them, exercising self-control and willpower" should work.

2 The impact of mental maps starts by cultivating moments of insight.

Large-scale behavior change requires a large-scale change in mental maps. This, in turn, requires some kind of event or experience that allows people to provoke themselves, in effect, to change their attitudes and expectations more quickly and dramatically than they usually would. As discussed, this can be the sharpening of incredible pain or inspirational insight.

For example, as I told you, I started my first business when two things collided. First, I disliked my boss at IBM and felt I could go no further there. At the same time, I was reading Paul Hawken's book, *Growing A Business*. As the founder of two companies (Smith

& Hawken and Erewhon), his insight inspired me to create my own company with the culture and values I wanted.

 # For insights to be valuable, they need to be generated from within, not given to individuals as conclusions.

This is true for several reasons, as discussed in the previous chapter. For one, people experience the adrenaline-like rush of insight only if they go through the process of making the connections themselves. The moment of insight is known to be a positive and energizing experience. This rush of energy may be central to facilitating change: It helps fight against the internal (and external) forces trying to keep change from occurring, including the amygdala's fear response. In addition, if the change was your idea, there is more of a chance you will stick to making it, even as doubt inevitably creeps in.

This is why I now realize that advice from outside consultants (like me) is rarely adapted unless the client internalizes it. They need to, in some way, discover it for themselves. For example, my client, Nikki (not her real name), wanted to create a new business that was an offshoot of the one she owned. So, we developed an outline of what the company could be. Only after she adjusted that vision to the way she could internalize it, was she able to move forward.

According to research by Jeffrey Schwartz, author of *The Mind & The Brain*, change is possible if you want it—you aren't at the mercy of genetically or predetermined brain activity. People can change their brain functioning with conscious attention and effort. In scientific terms, this is known as self-directed neuroplasticity.

The process starts by understanding mental maps, the neural connections which influence the reality we see or believe. For example, if we are given a pill for pain and don't know it's actually a sugar pill, we have the mental expectation that the medication will solve the pain. And the pain can still go away based on our beliefs. However, we can change our mental maps and connections to rewire our brains by experiencing new insights. Whenever we experience a new insight, new connections are formed.

But as we make those new connections that can lead to change, our brains may be fighting it through the amygdala's fear response as the brain detects an error between what is expected versus what actually is occurring. To negate the fear response, you need to "own" any change initiative and generate new insights from within. "People will experience the adrenaline-like rush of insight only if they go through the process of making connections themselves. The moment of insight is well known to be a positive and energizing experience," explain David Rock and Jeffrey Schwartz. "This rush of energy may be central to facilitating change."

As new connections are formed, "we need to make a deliberate effort to hardwire an insight by paying it repeated attention," write Rock and Schwartz. The amount of repeated attention given to an insight is known as attention density. Repeated, purposeful, and focused attention can lead to long-lasting personal evolution.

The following are tips for facilitating change through self-directed neuroplasticity, according to Rock and Schwartz:

1—**Awareness:** Become aware of a problem and what you'd like to change.

2—**Attention:** Focus your attention on implementing that change, so it becomes a reality.

3—**Volition:** At first, change will feel uncomfortable—the brain will want to continue repeating the patterns it has already learned. So, you need to have the will to want to make the change.

4—**Consistency:** You need consistent effort to create new neural pathways in your brain. Practice at least 15 minutes every day.

Seth Godin reminds us that there is magic in the countdown to form commitment. He writes:

"Thea von Harbou invented the countdown. 10, 9, 8...
It works.
It focuses the attention of everyone involved and ensures that we're truly alert for what's going to happen next.
It helps that the numbers go down, not up (because up might never end).

And it helps that as we get closer to lift-off, the tension goes up, not down.

But what really matters is this:

There's a commitment.

When we get to zero, we're actually going to do this.

The commitment has to happen before the countdown can."

Agile brain pathways for new habits.

Deborah Ancona, professor of management and organizational studies at MIT, and neuroscientist Tara Swart discuss how people can keep their brains agile and become better leaders. Just as athletes train their bodies to perform at an elite level, business leaders can achieve a competitive edge by understanding and improving the physical condition of their brains.

When people engage in the same habits, the neural pathways we use for those activities "become very stuck and deeply embedded, moving into deeper portions of the brain," says Ancona. "By the time we get to the age of 25, we just have so many existing pathways that our brain relies on, it's hard to break free of them."

When the brain feels like it is in danger mode, it cannot focus on the things required to create new neurons. Instead, it will travel along familiar pathways to mitigate risk. Also, to maintain brain flexibility, you need to practice healthy habits since your brain uses many of your body's nutrients, especially as it learns new behavioral patterns.

Neuroscientist Tara Swart says the best way to create new habits is: Replace your insecurities and anxieties with positive affirmations. Don't allow self-sabotaging thoughts to intrude your mind, and "meet [them] with a calm repetition of a mantra that contradicts [them]." For example, think about other changes you have successfully made to give you the confidence to make these new ones.

Make yourself accountable. Share your aims and ambitions with a mentor or a friend and ask them for their encouragement to keep you on track.

5 Take it easy.

Researchers Sheeran, Trafimow, & Armitage provide evidence that also suggests that intentions are more likely to be translated into action when respective behaviors are easier to perform by the brain). Goal difficulty is a function of the resources, ability, skills, cooperation, opportunities, and time and effort needed to realize the goal.

Whether or not a person acts is based on their intention to do so. Intentions are based on attitude ("It would be good for me to do X"), or there is social pressure to act ("Other people think it would be important for me to do X"). But whether or not an intention becomes an action ultimately depends on whether an action is easy to perform—and that is based on the opportunity or a person's ability and resources.

The ease or difficulty of a task is not necessarily based on the reality of the work but based on an individual's perception of how difficult they *think* it will be to perform the task. Further research says that a person's belief about the difficulty of acting is based on how much control they believe they have over behavioral performance. Mastery goals (which focus on developing a skill) tend to be easier to achieve than performance goals (which concentrate on outperforming others).

HOW TO BE A CHANGEMASTER

AM NOT MINIMIZING how hard change is. It involves taking risks, getting out of your comfort zone, and possibly losing whatever you already achieved. Plus, you have to fight against your own brain's instincts.

But change starts with taking small, patient, iterative steps. The key is just to start somewhere. Sometimes, almost anywhere will do. Forget the giant risky leaps. The key to making successful change is not making fatal mistakes along the way you can't recover from. Often, when looking back, we tout the changes we made as massive risks, but in reality, there wasn't one significant change but rather many small and incremental ones that led your company to a better place. It only appears that we took giant leaps when the story gets retold, and we bask in our success.

But the destination isn't the journey. And the narrative of the actual risks is up to us.

Seth Godin writes, "It's possible you've come to the conclusion that the destination you've chosen isn't for you. That being a pop star, a successful VP of accounting, or a receptionist with a secure position isn't a life you'd like to lead.

But don't confuse that with the journey. Maybe you'd be happy with finding the pot of gold at the end of your rainbow, but perhaps you don't want to suffer the discomfort, indignities, and effort it will take to get to that destination. Maybe you'd prefer an easier path. You'd happily accept the destination, but the truth is, the journey is too arduous to get there.

And don't confuse that with imagining the risks along the way. It may well be that you not only accept the destination, but you're also willing to endure (or delight in) the journey. However, your narrative of the risks and dangers is just too much to handle.

When we conflate the destination with the journey with the narrative of the risks, we have no hope of improving any of the three. So instead, we often push to throw out all three at once or embrace them all. But it's possible, with effort and planning, to make the journey more palatable or the risks feel more tolerable."

One of the dangers of change is pivoting too quickly. Entrepreneurs are impatient by nature. But if you pivot too fast, you may not have given the original change enough time to work. Also, your team will get whiplash and have a hard time adopting yet another change (and won't implement it since they think you will implement another change if they just wait).

Change Starts Here

1 Find the internal commitment to change.

There is no reason to pay for advice if you are not going to act on it. This doesn't mean always following the consultant's advice. But try to find a way to integrate it into your decision-making process. The process starts by understanding why you want to implement change and what will happen if you don't. You need to know what the cost of staying exactly where you are will be.

For example, I recently started to mountain bike after years of being a road cyclist. The sports are very different since your position on the bikes is quite distinct. On a road bike, it's all about speed. On a mountain bike, it's about stability. I decided to take a mountain biking class to teach me the correct positions and realized I had already developed bad habits. I had to relearn how to grip the handlebars and brakes with my fingers in the correct positions. This was a hard change to make since I was comfortable—and successful—the way I was doing it. But as my grip changed to the correct position, I became more adept at riding more challenging terrain.

Make small changes first.

Making radical departures from current practices are difficult to get your brain comfortable with, especially if your business is not a disaster. So, implement small pieces of advice first and measure the results before tackling more extensive changes. It is important to adopt several bits of advice, not just one, so you can judge the long-term outcome. This way, you can start to trust that the change will actually move you in the direction you want to go. For example, when riding my mountain bike, I first changed to the correct grip on the terrain I was comfortable riding on. Once I became more experienced and comfortable with that, I could use the new grip on more challenging parts of the ride.

 # Seek multiple sources of advice.

There is no single business guru out there and no one correct way to do things. Seek advice from several different sources to get a 360-degree view of the marketplace and your business. Consider assembling an informal board of advisors that meets quarterly to give you various points of view to better inform your own opinion.

Shift your point of view.

Forget radical changes. Start by slightly shifting your point of view. This way, the change is not so extreme that you can't return to where you were if this new approach fails. For example, in my mountain biking lesson, the instructors told me I was doing many things wrong. However, I did not try to change all of them at the same time. As I mentioned, I started with the handgrips and then implemented more changes after I got comfortable with the new approach. When my katas in karate need correction, I don't simultaneously work on properly positioning my hands and feet since that's too much change to make all at once.

 # Take action and commit to it.

Super trainer Jennifer Jacobs says it takes more than just desire to change; you also must take action. "You'll never find the perfect time to do whatever it is that you desire, but it's always the right time to start. Even if it's just one pushup, that's one more than you did yesterday. Take the simple approach to be better than you were yesterday. Simple to say, but [it's] challenging to be consistent on a daily basis to take action towards that goal. By committing to and taking action to do just one pushup often leads to more, longer workouts, [and] increased motivation."

Expect the change to be successful.

Forget failure and expect success! Formulate new mental maps of that change in your brain and where it can take you will help make this a reality.

 # Apply gentle pressure.

If you start overthinking or doubting yourself, apply a bit of pressure to take action. As Manish Patel, CEO of Brandify, says, "Pressure can bring out the best in you. Why do you think diamonds are so special?" Create that pressure on yourself, whether you are counting down from 10, or imagining yourself going live on television, or setting a deadline/timer to get yourself to move into action.

The 20 Steps to Making a Successful Change

I created this process to give small business owners the sense of control they need in order to enact change in their companies. This worksheet also provides you with a focused approach to accomplish that change. You can complete the steps as quickly or slowly as you want. But do them in order and don't skip any single step.

Check out the blank worksheet in the appendix. After reading this section, fill it out and start making your first change. As an example, I used a simple financial change that is a big issue for small businesses, but the worksheet enables you to start with any change you want.

PART 1:
BE THE CHANGE

1. What is the change you want to make?

Before you actually make a change, you first need to clearly articulate what that change is. Many people find this step difficult because they can't admit when something isn't right, and change is necessary. Instead, they're fighting with their brains for wanting to stay in the same place and do the same thing over and over again.

Changes are easier to make if they are specific, small, and incremental. To change, you need to start—somewhere. Almost anywhere will work. Remember, it's hard to make big changes all at once. When examined closely, most significant changes began as a series of small ones.

As Seth Godin says, "Even better than buying a new bicycle is adjusting the seat on your existing bike properly. That's because the height of the seat changes your power. It's the point of maximum leverage, responsible for aligning all of the forces you bring to bear on the process.

When we begin to think about our work, we tend to focus on the largest structures—what it looks like from the outside. But as we engage with the problem at hand, it turns out that our impact changes based on how we stand, what we believe, and the ways we interact with the systems right in front of us.

Get the strategy right, then implement small changes, repeated with persistence and generosity," he concludes.

For example, many small business owners do not conduct a monthly review of their financial statements. This is a bad practice since they're not getting financial insight into what's going on and cannot plan for the future. One common excuse is that the information is too overwhelming for them to understand. And accountants often struggle explaining financials to a non-numbers person. If you're one of these people, you can make a small change and start reviewing just your profit and loss statement every month with your accountant or bookkeeper. Have them explain it to you at a level you can understand.

2. How are you currently doing the thing you want to change?

To make a change, you need to clearly state what you are doing now compared to what you want to do. Just say it! It is critical not to judge yourself for your current behavior because, while it is not optimal, some part of it may work. Being hard on yourself will make any change you want to make that much more difficult.

For example, currently, I only review my profit and loss statement when my accountant reminds me. And even then, I don't understand what they are telling me, so I can't use this information to guide my company. So, without judgment, I have to admit I don't have the information required to run my business properly.

3. Why do you want to make this change?

The most common reason people change is that they are in so much pain and cannot stay exactly where they are. However, change can also be thrust upon you by outside forces that you accept. Or it can be internally motivated. Circumstances often force small business owners to make changes. For example, they may need to hire a new employee because the last one quit. Or they'll look for bigger office space because their company is expanding. Business owners pay taxes because the government will put them in prison if they don't.

In my example, I want to understand my profit and loss statement because no matter how hard I work or how much revenue I bring in, there is never have enough money at the end of the month to pay all my bills. So, I want to know why and what I can do to change that.

4. What will happen if you do not make this change? Be specific.

To enact actual change, there must be a painful consequence if you don't do it. If you don't think there will be any consequences if you don't change, you are less likely to make that change. Consider what the emotional, social or financial cost would be of not making the change. These are the two top ways people measure the cost of not changing: What will it cost me financially, or how much emotional stress will I feel?

In my example, if I don't start reviewing my financial statements, I won't be able to pay my bills. I won't understand why, even though my sales are increasing, I still won't have enough money at the end of the month. Not making this change could cost me tens of thousands of dollars, and I won't sleep worrying about it.

5. What inspired you to make this change?

A genuine desire for change must come from within. Of course, as I've noted, change can be forced upon you, but you are the only one that can make the change happen. The word inspired is used specifically here—inspiration is a mental stimulation that comes from deep inside yourself. Think about what is really forcing you to change? Why can't you live or move forward in your business without making this change?

In my example, I need to review my profit and loss statement since I don't have enough cash to grow my business. And I want to make more money and live with less pressure.

6. What makes you uncomfortable when you think of making this change?

One of the reasons people are reluctant to change is they fear the unknown. They're not only afraid to fail, but they may be afraid to succeed. As I've said, "The devil we know is better than the devil we don't." In other words, at least you understand your current problems and how you deal with them. You fear that making a change could bring on an entirely new set of issues that may be worse than what you are dealing with now. In so many cases, because of this fear, people stay precisely where they are at and don't make any changes.

In my example, my biggest fear in reviewing my financial statements monthly is that I will be even more confused about where to take my business with this new information. Or I may discover my business is in even worse financial shape than I thought, increasing my stress. Sometimes, ignorance can be more comfortable than knowing.

7. Who is the one person who can support the change? Why are they the right person for this job?

We are social beings and, for change to happen, we need support from other people whose opinions we value. This can be a friend or mentor who will keep you accountable for implementing a change but not judge you for the outcome (whether it's successful or not). When you have a new idea, want to brag about an achievement, or talk about a bad day, who do you currently turn to? Whoever they are, this person should not be afraid to hold you accountable for actions you said you would take and remind you of your commitments. Remember your joint expectations with this mentor will push you to make it a reality.

My mentors, Rieva and Rick, have always been good sounding boards for me. When I am unsure of the change I need to make, they advise me without judging me. I'm never worried about sharing my progress or lack of progress with them because I know they are there to help. In Chapter 10, I explain how to find the perfect mentor or support person.

8. What precisely can they do to support you in this change? Name a specific action.

Once you pick the person, define how do you want them to support your change. Should you check in with them by phone, text, video, or email? How frequently? Do you want them to reach out to you if they do not hear from you after a certain amount of time? Make sure they agree to the method and the frequency so supporting you does not feel like a burden to them. You must ask for what you need if the support is to be effective. Decide if you just want them to listen or give you honest feedback on your progress or lack of it.

In my example, I would like to email Rick about my progress and challenges once a week.

9. Reread these tomorrow and make any changes to your answers.

Stop! Focus and repetition are key for change and reinforcement. Review all your answers the following day to see if you want to adjust them. If you do, wait until the next day to review them again. Repeat this process until you do not have any changes to make.

Even though it may be tempting, do not skip this step! Only through refining and focusing on the change you want to make can you get it right. But remember, don't go for perfect since that does not work with change. In the beginning, the changes you make will not be perfect but will have to be refined over time.

PART 2:
MAKE THE CHANGE

10. What is the smallest step you can take to move toward this change? Be very specific.

According to a popular myth, big changes are made in one sweeping grand move. People love those types of stories because somehow it seems more heroic. As I've said, this is nonsense. Most changes happen in small, patient, iterative steps. Creating positive momentum in a new direction is critical to making changes.

For this part of the worksheet, pick a tiny step you can take to "move in the direction" of the change you want to make. It could be as simple as sending an email, making a call, or putting a difficult task on your to-do list.

In my example, I can ask my accountant or bookkeeper to review the sales and net profit from last month with me and compare it to the previous month. This is an excellent way to start small but still get the critical information I need to understand my profit and loss statements.

11. What positive affirmation or reward can you give yourself after you complete the first small step?

No matter how old we get, we're never far from the child we were who wanted a reward for doing something difficult. Reward yourself in the same way, especially after you complete an action that was uncomfortable for you. This reward counterbalances your brain's attempt to fight the discomfort. Remember, this is a reward for taking action, not necessarily being successful at it (at least the first time around).

I reward myself by indulging in my favorite sweet food treat—an almond vanilla RX energy bar.

12. Share the success or failure of this step with your mentor.

Don't pass judgment on yourself when you do this. Being too hard on yourself just increases your chances of quitting before actually making the change or not doing it at all

If you were unable to take the step you planned, ask your mentor for their ideas to help ensure it happens the next time.

13. After talking with your mentor, rate your success in accomplishing this step from 1 to 5 (lowest to highest). If the rating was not 4 or 5, what can you do better next time?

Be honest with your progress and rating. Consider asking your mentor to rate you as well.

14. How did your success (or failure) reinforce your inspiration to—or your fear of—change?

This step is not to criticize you but to learn from what happened. For example, were you more inspired to change or more fearful about changing?

15. What is the next smallest step you can take to move toward making this change?

Many people will have quit on the change by now. Keep going and think of the next smallest step to make toward the desired change. Remember, change is an iterative process that requires repetition and focus until it becomes a habit.

In my case, my accountant and I can now review the major expenses on my profit and loss statement and compare them to past results.

16. What positive affirmation or reward can you give yourself this time after completing this task to fight the discomfort of change?

My reward would be to go for a bicycle ride during work hours.

17. Once again, share the success or failure of this next action or step with your mentor or support person.

Don't give up on making this change until you have gone through all the steps at least twice. If you consistently fail to complete the steps, restart the process, but try changing something else that will be easier to accomplish.

18. After talking with your mentor, rate your success in accomplishing this step from 1 to 5 (lowest to highest). If the rating was not 4 or 5, what can you do better next time?

Be honest with your progress and rating. Again, consider asking your mentor to rate you as well.

19. How did your success (or failure) reinforce your inspiration to—or your fear of—change?

This step is not to criticize you but to learn from what happened. For example, were you more inspired to change or more fearful about changing?

20. What is the one thing that will help you not give up on making this change?

Don't give up on making this change until you have gone through all the steps. You may have to do this multiple times. If you consistently fail to complete the steps, restart the process, but try changing something else that will be easier to accomplish.

Note to readers: If you are eager to try this out for yourself, skip to the Appendix to start making your first change by filling out the worksheet.

Meet Some Small Business Owners Who Became ChangeMasters

Becoming a ChangeMaster is not about making significant sweeping changes all at once. It is about starting with a small initial change and then making another one until you leverage these multiple changes into something meaningful for your company. All those stories of people that made dramatic successful changes in their businesses are just stories.

A long-time client of mine, Marc (not his real name), wanted to leave his expensive shared office space on Madison Avenue in New York City and go virtual. He dreamed of spending more time in Florida and not be tied to the two-hour commute to the city every day from New Jersey. So, he made the move.

The pain that enabled this change was making a long daily commute just to be stuck inside a Manhattan office building instead of working outside or from his home office with a 12-foot commute from one room to another. So, he and his partners started this change by assembling the technology which would allow the entire company to work remotely. Then they let employees work a few days from home and hired people outside of the New York metro area. Finally, when this proved successful, they didn't renew their lease and transformed into a virtual company. Then, when the COVID-19 pandemic began, they were already working virtually when many other small businesses were trying to figure out how.

Many people make a change and become small business owners when there is no other choice. These "accidental entrepreneurs" often start an endeavor as a hobby and turn it into a full-time business when something in their lives changes. For example, while working for a professional soccer club, John (not his real name) started a part-time soccer training business. Then he was laid off, and his most obvious choice was to dive into running his training company full time. Business went so well the first few months he quickly expanded his offerings.

Other small business owners use accountability to make a change. For example, Arnie (not his real name) joined a small group within a business coaching company and committed to participating so he would not get distracted. Arnie says, "This time, I'm sticking with the change of being in a group, partly for the accountability part of it. My group keeps me accountable, in part, by using business tracking forms we must fill out and share. It is embarrassing to show up to our bi-weekly meeting and not have the forms filled out. Worst case, we'll get kicked out of the group if we don't do our homework—that's pretty strong accountability."

Many people literally change out of fear. Manny (not his real name) had an eye-opening visit to his cardiologist with negative results. It moved him to become a vegan like his wife. He changed his shopping and eating habits and did not buy meats, cheeses, or other dairy foods. Interestingly enough, in order to make the change, he allows himself a "cheat day" when he eats eggs for breakfast!

Or Janet (not her real name), for example, always positions every change as a trial run. She tells herself it's not permanent, and she can go back to the way it was. So, during the "trial" of moving her office back home, Janet treated problems as issues to solve rather than reasons to fail. She says, "I find change is easier to manage if I have a pre-defined out. Knowing there is an escape hatch allows me to be all-in on the change and do my absolute best to make it work."

CHAPTER 6

HOW TO BECOME A CHANGEMASTER FOR OTHERS

REMEMBER—YOU ARE A leader, or you would not be running a small business. People want to follow you and do what you do. It's much like imitating our mothers and fathers, who, in most cases, were the first leaders in our lives.

While helping small business owners for the past 20 years, I've discovered it is hard to get other people to change, especially if you struggle with that challenge yourself. Chances are that your team also struggles with this problem. Inertia usually keeps a business going in the same direction because "it's the way things have always been done" (and there has been some success). Employees keep doing things the same way they have always done them or how their predecessor did.

Before accepting that premise, however, you need to get to the root of the issue. When I was young, my mother cut off the ends of the pot roast before putting the pan in the oven. I asked her why and she replied, "Well, that is the way grandma did it." However, when I asked my grandma why she cut off the ends of the pot roast before putting it in the oven, she told me the entire pot roast would not fit in her small pan!

Things change (in your kitchen) and your life. You may start using new (pans or ovens) equipment. As the marketplace changes, business leaders must motivate their employees to change and evolve if they want their companies to continue to grow.

How to Create Change in Your Company

As the company's leader, you must establish the new goal or mission and explain clearly where the business is headed. You need to help your team, as Simon Sinek says, "Find their why." Employees will rally to make a change if there's a driving reason they can get behind. This doesn't mean you put it up to a vote. Running a small business is not a democracy; it's up to you to set the direction (with input from your team).

But you still need to answer the questions, "Why is it so critical to make this change now?" and "What does this mean for the company, the employees, and the customers?" Put another way, your team wants to know, "Why will this change make things better (and not worse) for the company, employees, and customers)?" Don't skip over these three targets. If you want your team to enact the change, they need to understand the benefits to all three, especially for their own career and personal goals. Employees get lost when missions and visions are unclear, or they don't know how it affects them. Articulate the parts of your company culture and principles that actually support the change. Your staff will also get lost if too many changes happen at once or if something changes every week. It freezes them in place as they just sit and wait for the next change.

For example, let's say you announce your lawn mower repair business is adding lawn mowing as an additional service. You reason that you're serving the same customer, and (in season) the grass constantly grows, so you will never lack work. You tell your team that instead of customers coming to you, the company will now go to the customers to sell your services and mow their lawns. You ramp up a marketing campaign to existing lawnmower repair customers and buy trucks to transport the mowers, but after a few weeks, there are few sales. You then decide this isn't working, so you decide to drop that service and instead add selling new lawnmowers to what your company does. You establish relationships with these new vendors, buy inventory, and train your team. You try this for a month, but don't make any sales. So go back to fixing lawnmowers. At this point, your team is exhausted trying to adapt to change and unlikely to embrace the next one.

Once you announce what you want to change, you and your team should determine the critical factors needed to achieve this goal in a set period of time successfully. Next, you need to decide the specific actions that must be completed to make the change a reality. This creates a roadmap to guide each person or department on what they must do for this to happen. Set small goals to start and gradually increase the difficulty and the frequency of the deadlines. Actually, beginning to change is one of the most challenging aspects of the whole process, and team members need to experience early "wins" to stay motivated and not get discouraged. This can establish a new momentum and eliminate inertia in the organization. Finally, let your team adjust the actions that need to be done for the change to occur. Giving them autonomy on which actions need to happen gets them invested in making it so.

For example, let's say you set a new goal to increase the retention rate of your current customers by 25%. You determine that one of the critical success factors (CSF) you need to reach this goal is having more customers use your service and then communicate their satisfaction to the budget decisionmaker. The team determines one of the additional actions they need to take to accomplish these CSFs is to monitor which part of the service customers use the most and increase content in that area. They also create an advocacy program to supply usage and results to the decisionmaker. The team then tracks results after a few months, which helps determine the next change.

It is also critical for you to find out what, if anything, your team fears when change is mentioned. As discussed, the natural tendency for most people is to keep things the way they are. Even if it is not working, people are comfortable in what they know rather than the unknown that change brings. Ask your employees what they need from you as the leader to support them in making this change. Ask them what connections they need to make with each other to ensure any changes actually occur.

You need to have a culture of change. It should be acceptable at your company to make small failures as a result of those changes. This reduces the fear (and any penalty) of transformation. If team members are afraid of change, it will never happen.

How to Create Change in an Employee

Running my companies and working with thousands of business owners has made me wonder whether employees (like most people) are truly capable of changing. Or are they who they are, and no matter what you do, they can't change? However, can effective leadership and the right culture help them become the best version of themselves? I have concluded that with the proper support, people can change.

You see it all the time in sports—a slumping superstar gets traded to another team for a fresh start and becomes a star again. Their former team kicks themselves for making the trade, but they don't realize that superstar would never perform at that level again on their team. Conversely, we've all called another company for references for a prospective new employee, and they sing that person's praises. But when we hire them, they are ineffective and do not work out. We wonder how they were ever successful at the last company.

Employees Reflect Their Company Culture

Employees tend to reflect the culture that surrounds them. That is why you always need to hire first for company culture fit and not skills or experience. This does not mean prospective employees don't need the skills to do the job, but they will never be effective if they don't fit into your company culture. For example, let's say that one principle of your culture is to give back to your community. So, even if you're hiring for a particular skill, it's critical to find an employee who already donates their time or money to a community cause. You can train people in skills, but you can't change what they value.

Leadership Fosters Change

Leaders and effective managers can inspire change through their standards and mentorship. We have all worked for bosses who we would follow anywhere and work harder for them than we've worked before.

Getting employees to change can be difficult, but it is doable over time. Here is where to start:

- Articulate their current behavior, which is ineffective or holding them back. Then, talk about how it hurts the company's overall goal, your customers, and their career (or anything else they care about).

- Clearly state the change you want them to make and how it will affect them. Then, ask them if they understand how making this change is in their best interest?

- Ask them what help they need to make that change and discuss how you will support them when they make it.

- Plot specific milestones and accountability points to keep the change on track.

- Follow up on the progress of the expected change. Review these steps if they haven't consistently embraced the change.

For example, suppose you have an employee who struggles with showing up for work on time. You can simply warn them and if they don't improve, fire them. But if they do a fantastic job for the company while they are at work, you can talk to them about how being late every day hurts the whole team's productivity. Remind them that it also costs them lost wages. Explain how if they arrive on time, the productivity of the entire department will improve, and they will be able to increase their compensation bonuses. Ask them what keeps them from arriving at work on time and what changes you can support to make an on-time arrival possible. Set a goal for them to arrive on time every day the following week and check on their progress. If they have not been successful, review these steps again.

Mission-Critical

Getting people to change and stand behind the company's goals and mission is critical. People are the most challenging part of growing and running a company, but they are also the most essential part. In many companies, without the people doing the work for you, you just have a job. In other words, if you can't go on vacation and have your company still earn money, it's a job. Remember, true leaders don't do all the work; they inspire others to do it for them.

Too many businesses start as hub-and-spoke organizations where the founder makes all the decisions. Unfortunately, as the company grows and managers are added, this structure never changes (although it might on paper). You must effect change in your managers to give them more decision-making responsibility so they can, in turn, inspire your staff.

Most small business owners are bad at doing this because they never learned to delegate. It is "easier" for them to do it themselves than go through the trouble of training others. In some ways, the owner thinks they are also being helpful. In addition, owners like to be busy and involved in every decision. When their boss is a micromanager, employees don't do what they are told. They know if they don't get the job done, the boss will do it for them. Leaders might wonder, "Why am I running out of time while my staff is running out of work?"

Staying on top of everything may seem like an effective way to run a company, but as the business grows, there is never enough time to do it all, no matter how hard the owner works. Instead, the leader must change and learn to delegate. Remember that authentic leadership is accomplishing the company's goals through others.

Delegate, Delegate, Delegate

The classic case study on delegating is recounted in the Harvard Business School paper on "Who's Got the Monkey" by William Oncken, Jr. and Donald L. Wass. The typical manager and employee interaction goes something like this:

Employee: Good morning; I am so glad I ran into you. I think we have a problem.

Manager: Really?

Employee: Yes, we are short of blue ribbon, and I am not sure how much we should buy for inventory since we are switching suppliers.

Manager: So glad you brought this up to me. I am in a rush right now. Let me think about it, and I will let you know.

What happened here? Following the Oncken and Wass theory, when the employee approached the manager, they had a problem (or "the monkey"), but when they parted, the problem (monkey) jumped over to the manager to solve. Monkeys are born because the manager knows enough to get involved but doesn't know enough to provide a solution on the spot. You have accepted responsibility from them to solve the problem, and you have promised to give a progress report on your solution. This is a guaranteed way to ensure that the manager always does the work while the employee doesn't.

If you are going to learn to delegate, you need to repeat one of my favorite phrases, "Not my circus, not my monkey," to the employee. According to Oncken and Wass, your management mantras must become:

- Your problem will never become my problem.

- If it does, you no longer have a problem, and I only help people with problems.

- After I help you, your problem will always leave with you

When employees have problems they want to discuss with you, insist they also present possible solutions. Remember, these transitions take time. You need to establish a two-way trust that comes with frequent, direct, and honest communication. In the beginning, this making this change is definitely more work than doing it yourself. However, ultimately, it will lead to company growth.

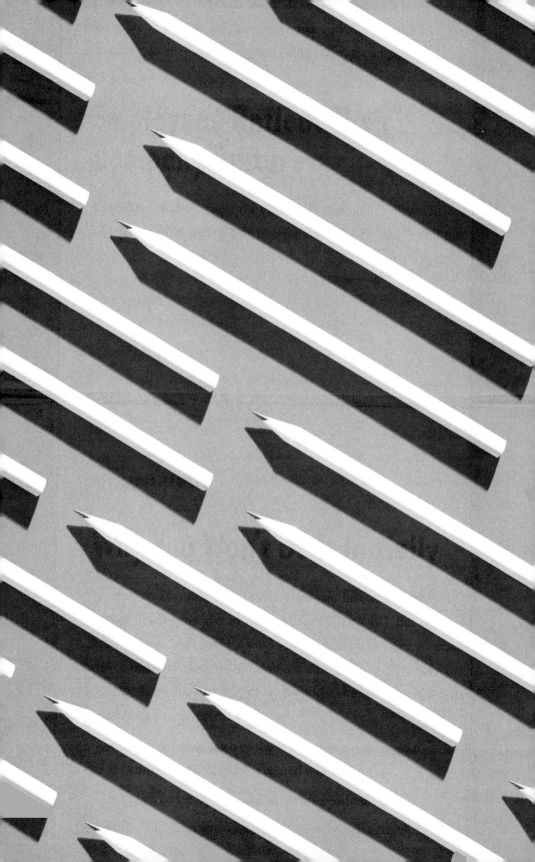

CHAPTER 7

HOW TO CREATE CHANGE IN SALES AND MARKETING

What You Do Now

You probably hate sales. You think it's "dirty" or "low" or "beneath you." Deep down, you may believe if you have the best product or service in the marketplace, it will "sell itself." This is just another lie you tell yourself for not selling consistently or having an ongoing process to do so.

The fact is the best products don't always sell the most, and the worst ones can be bestsellers depending on the circumstances and market strategy. For example, I think a lot of people would agree that Windows probably isn't the best personal computer operating system, and yet, it is the most widely proprietary one distributed. Microsoft achieved this success by getting their operating system on every personal computer distributed in the early days.

It's easy to get caught up in what I call the "Double Helix Trap". When things are slow, you mount a massive marketing effort, but as soon as sales pour in (as a result of that marketing), you pause your efforts to execute on the sales you made. This keeps revenues flat, and companies stuck in the same place.

Changing this "trap" is very difficult because most of us don't like to sell or market our products to people whose level of interest is unknown to us. Let's face it, like most of us, you are afraid of rejection. You take it personally. There are two principles you need to understand here before you can enact change. First, rejection is not personal. They are rejecting your product or service, not you. They may turn it down simply because they don't feel the intense pain your solution solves or don't have the money to solve that pain. Second, unless you constantly tell prospects about the pain you can solve, you will never be top-of-mind when people are ready to buy. Most prospects have a "maybe pile," according to Robin Creasman, a mentor of mine. When they want to buy something, they list three places in their minds where they can make that purchase or three people they can get a referral from. To be in that "maybe pile," you need to have consistent outreach, or you will never get chosen.

Where to Start to Make the Change

To solve this, you need to convert to a systematic marketing and sales process where the things you don't have time to think about automatically happen because you are busy doing other company tasks. This is hard to implement because it takes a lot of thinking and planning to initially set it up. But the good news is once it is established, it just operates, and the sales pipeline stays full.

It is essential to learn the difference between selling and marketing. Most small business owners say they hate to sell. This is not true. What people hate to do is market. Most people love selling to an identified prospect once they know they can solve their problem. What they hate to do is find "suspects" and turn them into prospects.

Suspects are targeted companies that have the problem your product or solution solves. For example, a vendor that sells customer relationship management (CRM) software (like Thryv or Zoho) might look for companies that need to keep track of and expand their customer contacts (people who have the problem they solve). Most companies of any size should be a suspect for them. But a prospect is a suspect who has "raised their hand" and said to the company in some way (like returning a phone call or email) that they need CRM software. In this case, they have been using Excel to track their suspects and prospects or another CRM system that does not meet their current needs. Those are the companies that have a higher probability of becoming future customers

This is precisely what marketing is all about. You need to market your business and its solutions constantly and consistently to your suspects, prospects, and current customers, so you are there when they're ready to buy. Unfortunately, this is where the sales and marketing strategy of most companies fails. Most small business owners spend a lot of time marketing and selling to two types of companies:

1. **Selling to current customers.** This is a good target since conventional wisdom says it is easier to get additional business from current customers than find new ones. Also, it is an opportunity to turn these customers into evangelists and have them refer new prospects. This is an integral part of sales. There is nothing as powerful as a great referral from another

client. As customer management consulting firm Peppers & Rogers labels it, you become their "trust agent." That means you get to bypass the building-credibility-and-credentials stage and go directly to "When can you start?" This is the fastest way to build your business.

2. **Selling to past prospects.** Unfortunately, other small business owners spend a lot of time trying to sell to past prospects. These people never became customers and long ago stopped returning phone calls and emails.

Business owners need to spend much more time marketing to suspects and converting prospects into customers. These two groups are the future sales that will feed your pipeline. However, you need to market to these groups differently.

How to Analyze:

Start with Suspect Marketing

Your suspect list is large. It consists of anyone whose business problems your company can solve. In most cases, the total universe is hundreds of thousands or millions of companies or individuals. Since it is not economical to directly sell to each suspect individually, the goal is to get them to somehow "raise their hands" and identify themselves as a prospect, as stated earlier. Following are five tactics for suspect marketing success:

1. **Advertise:** If you do not have a large budget, use trade journals or online publications where you can narrow the list of suspects for a reasonable amount of money. This is a lot less expensive and more targeted approach than buying ads in traditional publications. Never advertise just one time in a publication. To ensure you get maximum results, place as many ad insertions as you can in targeted magazines or newspapers at a size your budget can afford. Buying more insertions at a smaller display size is better than buying a full-page ad you can only afford to run once. No matter what size you can afford, a minimum of three insertions for repetition is required. Make every ad trackable so you can determine its return.

2. **Direct email:** Buy lists of "opt-in" names from a broker and use a marketing email system to track who opens the emails and who clicks through to your website. This may seem a bit sneaky, but today's technology allows you to do this. Suspects clicking through on your email is the equivalent of "raising their hands" so you can begin to get traction with them. Think about the appropriate follow-up activity for each of these leads so they can be nurtured to a sale.

3. **Paid search:** Use Google AdWords on search or Facebook, Twitter, Instagram, and LinkedIn on social media to promote your business. You only pay when a suspect clicks through to your website. The best part about paid search is that your company can set its own budget and even target a local area. You decide how high you want to be on the search list (by

paying more) and how much money you want to spend each month. However, this is very difficult and can be expensive to effectively do it alone without an expert's help.

4. **Trade shows:** If you have a large enough budget, pick a few targeted shows to exhibit at. Consider sending a pre-show offer to attendees to incentivize them to come by your booth. If you are bootstrapping your business and can't yet afford to exhibit, it can be almost as effective to walk the trade show floor, collecting cards from attendees. You could also try to participate in a conference panel to get increased exposure. Follow up and email everyone you met and nurture these relationships as described above.

5. **Become an expert:** Write an article about something of value in your industry and get it published in print and/or online media. Companies buy from experts, and these external media sources will give you additional credibility with the suspects you do not know—they act as "trust agents." You can also repurpose the article as content on your own website or a newsletter (get permission, of course).

Continue with prospect marketing

Your prospect list is a dialed-down version of your suspect list. It is much smaller because the companies on this list fulfill three requirements: 1) You know they have a problem you can solve, 2) They have the money to solve the problem, and 3) You know the decisionmaker.

In most cases, this universe will consist of 10 to 1,000 companies/individuals, depending on the size of your company. You should try to contact each of these prospects individually, as consistently as possible through a variety of media so you can be there when their pain is so great that they must buy something—which may as well be from you! The following four tactics will help you connect with these prospects:

1. **Direct sales:** Call and email your prospects to check the status of their pain or need and let them know about your solution for it. There is nothing wrong with being aggressive—just don't become annoying. What is the difference? Keep track of the last time you contacted them and when they called you. Don't call more than twice to every unanswered call from them. If those two calls aren't returned, you can call every few weeks for a month or so. No answer or reply? Then you no longer have a prospect, and you need to move on to other interested prospects.

2. **Referrals:** The right customer for you may not be the prospect themselves but could be someone they know. Stay in front of the prospect, and they will be thinking of you the next time an associate of theirs can use your services. As stated previously, this "trusted referral" is the most powerful sales tool in business. You can always ask for referrals by saying, "Do you know

anyone else who my solution may help?" You will be surprised by how helpful a satisfied customer can be!

3. **Direct email or postal mail:** This is a very cost-effective technique since your number of prospects is limited. Send them industry information or articles of interest so they will continue to see you as an expert who can solve their problems. As with the other tactics, it's critical to consistently market to your prospects (at least weekly). It is not something to do once, when you run out of leads, or when your work dries up.

4. **Start to educate them:** Use a systematic marketing plan where your company brings expert value to prospects and customers on a weekly or biweekly basis. (You're not selling features here.) Before the internet, experts said a potential customer needed seven brand reinforcements until they remembered that company. Now, with the onslaught of inbound information targeting every customer, it takes 21 reinforcements. With no geographic boundaries and overnight shipping, every company that does what your business delivers is a competitor.

Customers buy from people and companies they know, like, and trust. It is critical to stay in contact with a potential customer, so you are part of that "maybe pile" when a customer is ready to buy. This is not done by bombarding them with new product offers, discounted prices, or seasonal specials. Most prospects will ignore those offers if they do not have a current need. What the potential customer wants instead is something of value that solves the problems they face every day. The internet may be filled with information, but it is still hard to find relevant information even using great search engines. This is where you can highlight your brand by sending or mailing something of value to the prospect every month.

The First Steps

Here are some ideas on what to communicate about:

- Did they just reach a significant milestone? Congratulate them or just send a message noting the achievement. This shows the prospect you are interested in them.

- Are you both attending the same trade show or conference? Suggest a meeting so you can connect in person.

- Point out a recent article, tool, or book that was valuable to you. This demonstrates you are knowledgeable and can be counted on to provide expert information.

- Identify a resource or make a connection for them to show you want to help their business beyond just selling your products or services.

You know you need to stay in front of your customers. And now you have some ideas on how to do that. But, first, you need to get them to open that email, and that starts with an intriguing subject line. In fact, 80% of the reasons someone opens an email is because of the subject lines. Here are some examples:

- "Saw this and thought of you."

- "I know you appreciate a good resource."

- "I have an idea for you."

- "Here is a great connection for you."

Content examples for specific industries include:

- HVAC: How to Keep Your Home More Energy Efficient

- Garden Shop: When Is the Right Time to Plant Tulips?

- Auto Repair: Will That Dent Rust?

- Insurance Agent: Why You Need Long-Term Care

- Plumber: The Biggest Danger in Your Home

The content needs to consist of single subjects, not a long, complicated newsletter. With the flood of inbound information today, prospects don't have time to read these, and companies have difficulty assembling so much content in one place.

If you use text marketing, your texts should be no more than 50 words, with a single hyperlink to the additional content.

Reach out weekly or biweekly. Don't get discouraged. It takes at least three months to form this habit. If you have 100 prospects or customers that need to be contacted, doing five a day will get you to the goal. Remember, promoting your brand with additional value should be a daily task—not something that just gets done when sales are lagging.

Why You Won't Do It Initially

It's hard to assemble any system when you first start. The objection of time always gets in the way (see Chapter 10). But remember, if you want to build a solid sales pipeline, you need to make this change. The second objection is always that you don't have any content. Businesses ask me, what should I write about in 300- 500 words? Start with these ideas:

- One article on each of the five biggest problems your customers face (and the related solution)

- A success story you have had with a customer

- A feature on your employees and what makes them interesting

- How, and why you started your business

You can find freelancers to write articles for you inexpensively (less than $50 an article) on sites like Upwork or Fiverr. However, make sure you edit those posts carefully because often, you get what you pay for.

Take These Next Steps Instead

Educate, don't sell: In his book, *To Sell Is Human: The Surprising Truth About Moving Others*, author Daniel Pink says selling is far from dead; rather, it is evolving. He insists companies can be more successful if they focus on the act of persuading others rather than the standard technique of always working toward the close. People no longer want to be sold products or services—they want to be educated about them.

This is a considerable distinction. With the internet, prospects can do their own research about your products and their features before contacting your company. In addition, they can discover what other people say about you and what it is like to do business with you. As a result, prospects are increasingly deleting or disregarding all the marketing messages they are bombarded with about your product's features and how wonderful life will be if they only buy it. Instead, use your branded marketing messages to educate them on how you and your product can actually help them instead of constantly touting your features.

Build trusted relationships: As I discussed, people prefer to do business with people they trust. This is now being personified with companies. To build trust, every business needs to think about the value and expertise they bring to help customers solve their problems, not the products they can sell to them. Position your company as an expert in "curing" specific pain points, and customers with that pain will come looking for you to buy your solutions.

A trusted relationship also increases that customer's lifetime value and profitability. It offers you the opportunity to expand the amount of business you do with them—to sell more products to the customer. For example, in 1994, Amazon started selling books. Once they established in the marketplace that they could reliably (meaning trustfully) deliver these books on time, they expanded to selling more other consumer goods. I even once bought my kayak on Amazon, which included free shipping! In 2020, I ordered from them over 350 times! If your educational technology company sells reading tools, your current customers may contact you to find out where they can find writing tools. Or, if you currently sell reading tools for K-5 grades, customers may want you to have a product for 6-12 grades.

But don't rush the trust: Most small business owners are passionately impatient. They can't wait to tell customers about their fantastic products/services. However, to first establish trust, it takes discipline not to start selling right away. When I visit a new prospective company, I never sell them anything the first few contacts. Instead, I begin by determining how I can help them. I know that if I do this, they will want to find ways to work with me. This process could take months or years.

Remember, business relationships take more time to build than personal ones. Unfortunately, many companies don't have the patience to establish a relationship with a customer before trying to sell them something. John Jantsch, the founder of Duct Tape Marketing, describes a systematic approach to building trustful relationships as a wheel with seven steps:

1—**Know:** Get to know who the customer is and what problems they need to solve. Any research you do before approaching the customer will always impress them. It will also enable you to ask better questions and find out what the customer truly needs.

2—Like: The prospect hears good things about your company in the marketplace and from their peers. Monitor your online reputation to listen to what others are saying about your business. Thank supporters gracefully, and it will subtly encourage them to keep complimenting your company.

3—Trust: At the start, provide help at no fee, so they begin to see your company as a source. At this stage, expect nothing in return. This does not mean giving away "the secret sauce" but rather "a taste" of the help you offer. Most customers do not expect something for nothing on a long-term basis.

4—Try: Let the customer try your product or service without any penalties. If they do not like it, they can return it. As an example, consumer catalog company Hammacher Schlemmer has a no-questions-asked return policy over the life of the product. Even though they sell at the highest price in the market, this policy encourages consumers to check out their unique products.

5—Buy: The customer makes their first real purchase once the first four steps are completed. This sale should be for a profit since the customers see the value. Making a profit also ensures that your company has the money to invest in the first four steps.

6—Repeat: The customer enjoys the product, so they buy it again and again. This is where the upfront investment becomes very profitable for the company, and the customer's lifetime value can increase exponentially.

7—**Refer:** The customer enjoys the product so much they refer friends who may be interested in a purchase. This is the most powerful marketing anywhere because an unknown company with a referral can go from "who are you?" to "how can I buy?"

Reputation marketing is getting all the buzz right now. According to the "Nielsen Global Trust Survey for Advertising Report," 92% of people trust recommendations from people they know. This is to be expected since personal referrals have always been powerful. But more important, consumers trust 70% of the opinions they read online from people they don't know.

In their Trust Index, these results beat the trust levels of company-branded websites (58%) and online ads (33%). In other words, reputation is more important than your company's brand or its direct paid advertising. Therefore, it is critical to pay attention to what people are saying about your company online. This can be as simple as responding respectfully to review sites like Yelp and Tripadvisor or tracking what people write on social media and online blogs. In addition, use free tools such as Google Alerts, so you know when a new review is posted.

While it may be tempting, never ignore the negative comments customers write about your company. Rather, view it as a gift since up to 90% of disgruntled customers will say nothing directly to the company. Instead, they will sulk away and never buy from that company again. However, they will continue to retell the story of their bad experience. I have retold a story of poor service at The Great

American Bagel hundreds of times (and here it is again). When I ordered a dozen sliced bagels, they wanted to charge me 5 cents extra to slice each one. I did not express my outrage at the time, but I have repeatedly retold this story.

Remember that no news is not always good news. As previously stated, dissatisfied customers complain frequently but not directly to you. According to the Harvard Business Review, 25% of happy customers are likely to say something positive about their customer service experience, but 65% are likely to speak negatively about it if they had a bad experience. In addition, 23% of customers who had a positive service interaction told 10 or more people. However, 48% of customers who had negative experiences told 10 or more people.

So, while customers are more likely to complain, you should see this as a positive opportunity. First, they have taken their valuable time to offer feedback directly to your company (or via another channel). Then you get a chance to turn around their negative experience. Surveys show that dissatisfied customers whose problems are fixed become even more loyal to the company than if they'd never had difficulties at all. You also get valuable feedback about things many other customers likely experienced but never mentioned. Track this continuously since customer service is a moving target, changing every month.

Listen and respond. Listen carefully to make sure you understand customers' concerns. Respond with empathy and vow to do better next time. Try not to find blame or hide problems that develop. Instead, ask customers for their suggested solutions. Get back to them on how you plan to resolve any issues. Then collect all these concerns so you can spot an overall trend within the company. You may not get a dissatisfied customer to buy again, but other prospects will see how you handle issues when things go wrong. This will encourage them to take the risk of purchasing your product.

How to Measure Successful Change

- How many times have you created and sent suspects, prospects, and customers new content this month?
- Are you tracking the results of the content that you send?
- How do you keep track of prospects?
- Is your sales pipeline growing?
- What stage is each of the prospects in?
- What is your close rate?
- What is your customer retention rate?
- Are you looking at your online reviews daily, and do you respond to the good and bad ones?

CHAPTER 8

HOW TO CREATE CHANGE IN MANAGING YOUR MONEY

What You Do Now

Money is hard for a lot of people. Difficult to talk about, earn, spend, and track it. People grow up with money-handling habits that are hard to change. For example, my parents always fought about money. When I was eight, I stayed up late at night trying to dream up ways to earn money so my parents would not argue anymore. I never did, but they stay married for 60 years, still talking about their issues about money.

Some people track and budget every penny. Others never balance their checkbooks. Small business owners bring all these habits into their professional lives when they start running their own companies. I always see their financial habits at home reflected in how they manage (or don't manage) their business finances. It has always fascinated me how some entrepreneurs running large companies don't have any interest in or are afraid to look at their company's finances. They seem to want to just rely on others.

Even though they may have a bookkeeper or accountant that bills customers, collects their money, and pays the bills, they never formerly review their financial statements. This is because so many of them are sure they know what is going on financially in their companies. They are typically wrong, and more than likely, they are just afraid to look. For example, one owner told me he was making a 90% gross profit margin; it really was 40%. Another said she made a net profit of 20%; she actually lost money that year. Others believe that they don't have to worry about the numbers as long as they have money in their bank accounts to pay their bills (and maybe themselves). They just hope to keep selling more to cover whatever happens next.

Many small business owners never learned to read financial statements and seem to be getting along just fine without them. Once a year, they bring in their accountant who tells them what they need to know. You don't ask her for help because she doesn't explain them well, or she makes you feel stupid when you ask a question. You are not even sure how these statements relate to running a business. You ultimately brush it off since you think you have a good idea of the "real numbers" in your head. As a result, you make all your business decisions blindly.

Your financial decisions are ruled by emotions. You do what feels right. This means either feeding your own ego or taking care of the company's squeaky wheel (a vendor, customer, or employee). This leads to borrowing and spending money based on poorly defined projected results, getting you into overwhelming debt.

You think business success is about revenue, not cash flow. You only focus on the top sales number. As long as this number keeps growing, you think your business will be successful. You believe that ultimately some of this money will trickle down to your own pocket. This isn't how being a successful small business owner works.

Ultimately, the cash profit drives the company's value to increase your personal wealth or the company's sale value.

You don't share any financial information with your employees. You see it as paradoxical. Will disclosing information that shows the company earning a lot of money make employees jealous? Will they then ask for raises? Alternately, if the company has financial problems, will employees worry and start looking for other jobs?

Where to Start to Make the Change

You first must establish what your specific financial goals are. Here's an example: "I want to have sales of $5M next year with a gross margin of 60% and a net profit of 20% so I can take $1M out of the company." Again, these are specific targets to hit in all the key financial metrics.

Start the process by finding out exactly what your annual results were last year. This may be in your profit and loss statement or on your latest tax return. Either way, build your projection on what you have done in the past and what you will do differently in the future (more products, more people, more customers, reduced costs) to get there this year.

If you do not understand how to read the basic balance sheet, profit and loss statement, or cash flow statements, reach out and get some help. I have an MBA from Northwestern University and once lost $1 million from the sale price of a business because I couldn't understand these simple financial tools. This is not something I am proud of but remember you are in good company in financial statements confused you. Help can come in the form of your accountant, books, or information on the web. If you have never learned to read these statements, it does take training since they often are not "user-friendly" or intuitive. Like so many other things, financial statements have their own lingo.

Commit to reviewing the accuracy of these statements every month and understand what they tell you about what happened in your business (and what it can mean for next month). Numbers have power—the power to make the best decision you can to beat your competitors.

How to Analyze

Learn how to read a profit and loss statement (also called an income statement): Get over your fear of the numbers. A financial statement shows the revenue, expenses, and profit of a business over a period of time. Following are the basic components:

- **Revenue:** Your sales, which come from customers that buy your products/services

- **Cost of goods or services (COGS):** The direct cost of producing the product or service the business sells; could be raw materials or labor

- **Gross profit:** The difference between sales and cost of goods; also known as the gross margin

- **General expenses:** Rent, people, insurance, utilities, telephone, travel, etc.

- **Net profit:** The difference between gross profit and general expenses; taxes and depreciation are typically deducted from net profit

Learn to read a balance sheet: This is the "book value" of your business at any given point in time. It also measures the ability of a company to pay its debts. Following are the basic components:

Assets: What the company owns. This can include:

- Cash: How much money the company has in the bank
- Accounts receivable: The value and age of the money that is owed to the business
- Inventory: The value of the inventory
- Fixed assets: Equipment, computers, and property

Liabilities: What the company owes. This can include:

- Accounts payable: The money the business owes vendors
- Loans: The money the company owes banks and other sources

Owners' Equity: The assets minus the liabilities. This can include:

- Stock: Paid-in capital
- Retained earnings: Profit retained in the company since the start

Here are three other measurements which reveal important information about your business:

1—The quick ratio (or the acid test) on the balance sheet: This is the business's current assets (cash, cash equivalents, accounts receivables) divided by current liabilities. A favored metric of banks, the quick ratio is a measure of the financial stability of a business. In most industries, the quick ratio should be greater than 1, which shows that the company has more cash available than the money it owes. Conversely, when the ratio falls below 1, it means your business may not be able to meet its financial commitments.

2—The business's sales-close ratio in your customer relationship management system (CRM): Of all the proposals your business sends, how many do you win? This is a critical number since it should not be too low or too high. If it is too high, either your business is not talking to enough prospects, or your prices are too low. If it is too low, you may not be qualifying your prospects enough before preparing proposals for them.

3—Your 10 most important customers: While this data is available on your profit and loss statement, you can rank your most important customers not only by revenue but also by referrals, the additional products they buy, the feedback they give, retention, or their superior brand power.

The First Steps

Run the profit and loss statement on a cash basis for last month from your financial system. What is essential to know is if the company made a cash profit (revenue collected is greater than bills paid). Alternately, download your last bank statement. Do you have more or less cash at the end of the month? At the end of the month, companies with cash profits can reinvest in building the company or pay it out to the owner.

Why You Won't Do It Initially

Looking at the numbers will be hard since you may be afraid of what the actual numbers say, especially when they are not in sync with what you thought in your head. This can be a real shock to the system. Often, after reviewing the financial statements, everything you ever thought about your business needs to be reset. This alone may keep you from reviewing the financial statements because you want to avoid any change that brings bad news. But remember, just because you don't know about "bad news" doesn't mean it's not there.

Take These Next Steps Instead

Track your numbers monthly and see the truth about your company's financial situation. Then, put together an executive review of key numbers, which are a subset of the financial statements. These should include:

- What were sales?

- What was the gross profit (sales minus direct cost of sales)

- What is the cost of overhead that involves people?

- What is the cost of overhead that doesn't involve people?

- What is your net profit (sales minus all expenses)?

- If you have inventory, how quickly does it turn? I.e., how long does the average product stay on the shelf (and eat up cash flow)?

- What is the quick ratio of the company that determines its short-term ability to pay its bills?

Put together a budget. Many accounting programs like QuickBooks, NetSuite, or SAP will allow you to migrate last year's results to next year's budget plus a percentage for growth. Budgets are an essential part of financial management, but many small business owners use this tool wrong. They set an annual budget but then adjust it every month if their results do not match. Stop doing this! Set a budget before the beginning of a fiscal year. Compare results, and only reset the budget at midyear. Budgets are useless if they get reset to match results every month.

How to Measure Successful Change

There is power in measuring success through objective numbers. These will be found on the profit and loss statements, balance sheets, and cash flow statements. The next step would be to compare it to the same period last year. The value of financial statements increases when you compare them to reports from another period of time or your projected budget.

Depending on your objectives, make the comparisons on these statements between:

- This month and last month
- This month/year compared to your budget
- Year-to-date this year vs. the previous year

You can also take this five-minute financial health test every quarter. I set this up because many small business owners have difficulty evaluating the financial health of their company monthly. They are not trained in reading financial statements.

Here is an easy assessment to use regularly and compare to previous time periods. It is not meant as a method to bypass reviewing the financial statements but as another means to measure your company's financial health.

1—Does your small business have positive or negative cash flow?

What this means: Do you have more or less cash at the end of the month?

Where to find it?

- Bank Statement. Look at the beginning cash balance and the ending cash balance. Do you have more or less at the end of the month?

- Cash Flow Statement from your accounting system. Look at the beginning cash balance and the ending cash balance. Do you have more or less at the end of the month?

If you have more cash at the end of the month, add one point to your total.

2—What is your current ratio?

What this means: It's the total current assets divided by the total current liabilities.

Where to find it?

- Your Balance Sheet from your accounting system.
- If it is greater than 1, add one point to your total.

3—Do you have monthly annuities for revenue?

What this means: Your business gets repeat revenue automatically every month from a subscription or contract without having to sell to a new customer.

Where to find it?

- The revenue or sales line on your profit and loss statement
- If you have annuity revenue, add one point to your total.

4—What percent of revenue is your gross profit?

What this means: Revenue (sales) minus Cost of Goods or Cost of Service.

Where to find it?

- Your Profit and Loss Statement from your accounting system
- If your gross margin is higher than 50%, add one point to your total.

5—More fixed vs. variable expenses?

What this means: Fixed expenses are usually all the expenses in your business except those directly related to the cost of providing the product or service you sell—for example, rent, marketing, internet service, and travel.

Where to find it?

- Profit and Loss Statement
- If fixed expenses are less than 20% of sales, add one to your point total.

Evaluate your total point score:

- **4 or 5: Congratulations!** Your small business is healthy and well-positioned for the year. Grow on!
- **3: At risk!** Key financial parts of your small business need to be improved. You are vulnerable to changes in the market.
- **1 or 2: Danger!** Too many parts of your business are unhealthy, and your company risks going bankrupt. Find Help!

Here are more tiny financial habits for success

- Invoice weekly or more frequently
- Limit customer credit
- Collect payments faster
- Pay vendors on time with a credit card
- Minimize inventory and maximize usage
- Make more expense variable
- Guard your cash jealously

- Only borrow money for quantifiable returns

One of the best financial measurements of change is how much you actually pay yourself. Unfortunately, so many owners pay themselves last. Mike Michalowicz, the author of Profit First, says, "One of the best financial measurements of change is how much you can pay yourself, without draining the business. While many of us entrepreneurs started our small businesses to do good in the world, we also did it to provide for ourselves, our families, and our communities. Let me be very clear: You have a responsibility to be profitable. It is the only way you can provide for yourself and others, and it is the only way your business can continue to serve our world. You more than deserve to make money ... you must."

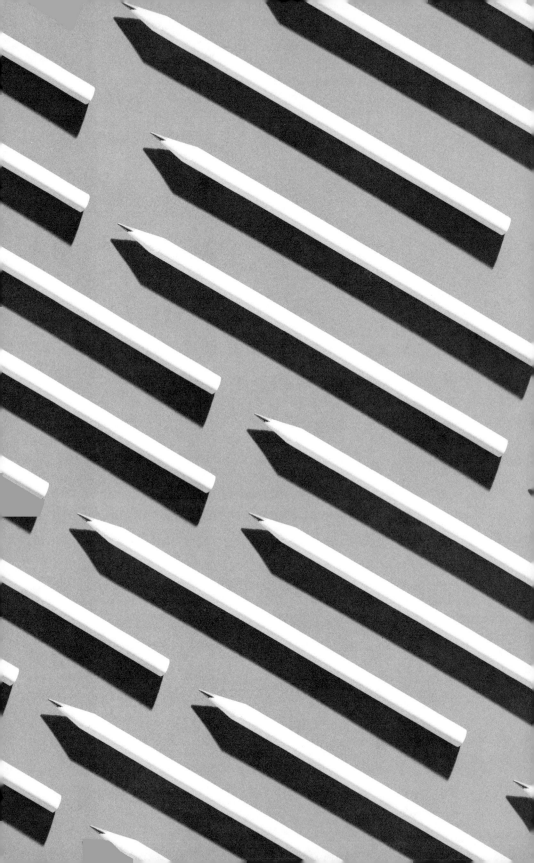

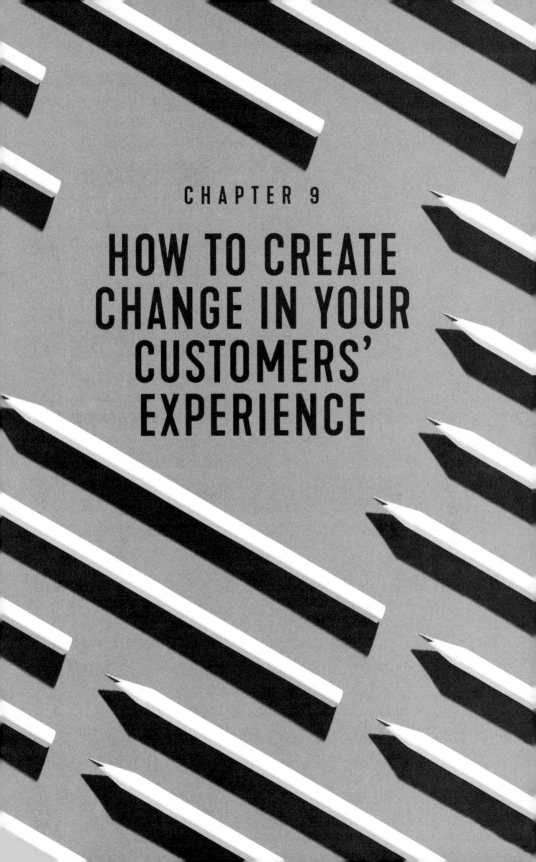

CHAPTER 9

HOW TO CREATE CHANGE IN YOUR CUSTOMERS' EXPERIENCE

What You Do Now

There is a deep, dark secret many small business owners do not want their customers to know. It conflicts with almost every small business's mission and goal—to love your customers and try **to provide** them with the best possible experience. Unfortunately, many small business owners are living a lie. The truth is that many spend a lot of time hating their customers because they feel they are too demanding, ignorant, or unreasonable. If most business owners could find a successful business to run that had no customers, they would do it!

Realistically, it is hard to always love your customers. They can be difficult. They can be ungrateful. But in the end, they are paying you to solve a difficult problem they can't fix for themselves. So, if you want to stay in business, you need to serve them the best way you can. Remember, they are coming to you because they have a problem. If they did not have issues, you would not have a business.

For small business owners, this means, while you're watching the front door, don't leave the back one open. Too many owners are so focused on bringing new customers in the front door that they leave the back door wide open, watching them go because of a poor customer experience. They spend all their resources on attracting new customers and don't think about keeping the ones they have. In fact, many focus all their sales and marketing energies and budgets on finding and selling new prospects and forget about the lifetime value of a customer. Remember how expensive it is to get new customers versus keeping the ones you have. We have all heard the business axiom that bringing in a new customer costs seven times more than retaining an old one, but we rarely behave that way.

Many small business owners think customer service is a necessary evil and place no value on servicing existing customers. Some even think the people who contact them only want to complain or get something for free. Therefore, they provide the minimum service in order not to subtract from the company's profits.

We'd all like to match Amazon's customer service model, but we don't have the resources to do that. Unfortunately, many of us think all consumers expect this, so we simply stop focusing on customer service when we can't make this type of investment.

However, the customer experience is more important than ever. The hard truth is no one wants to just buy your stuff or your service. They want to have an authentic and personal customer experience with your business. That means the goalposts have moved, and if you are going to grow your business, you have to move with them.

Where to Start to Make the Change

Examine your customer acquisition strategy: What does it cost to acquire a new customer compared to growing the ones you have? Many small business owners are reluctant to invest money to get new customers. But if you could make $100 gross profit off a customer, would you give me $10 to keep them? All-day probably.

Stop the search: While there may be more ideal customers out there, it is impossible to look for them all simultaneously. If you are dissatisfied with all your current customers, then you may be in the wrong business. Instead, prioritize your customers. Stop complaining about the customers that are contributing to your profitable business. Rather, weed out the few that are real problems or are unprofitable for you to continue to do business with.

Get interested now: To build a business, you must be sincerely interested in your customers' success. Here's how:

- Find out why your customers buy your products or services the first time and continue to. What pain does it solve for them? What is its value? Explore what they think about doing business with your company. Include the good, the bad, and the truly ugly. Listen to their concerns, act, and give feedback.

- Build a culture of like. All your negativity around customers builds a culture of dislike and dissatisfaction within your company. It is a cancer that spreads. This may first manifest in your employees. Do they have a negative or disparaging tone when talking to customers over email, chat, or in-person? That can grow into an "us against the customers" (or the world) mentality. This type of negative energy is not part of building a winning culture. It's very easy to pay lip service to customer satisfaction. After all, no companies publicly advertise "we hate our customers and want nothing to do with them." But it's actually frightfully easy to create a company culture that seems to be apathetic, or even hostile, toward its customers. To be successful, you must genuinely have a passion for helping your customers and not view them as the enemy. Remember, they pay you money to solve their pain, so do not be surprised or angry if they come to you with it.

- Of course, your employees play a big part in creating satisfied customers. If your current team does not have the skills to accomplish today's job (or that of the near future), begin looking for replacements. If employees are poisoning the company culture, they must be let go immediately, regardless of their contributions.

- Hire employees who believe in your values. Despite what many people think, most employees are not mercenaries out looking for the best paycheck. Most people are interested in doing meaningful work for a company they can believe in. Develop clear values for your business, stand by them, and hire employees who agree with them. That way, they will interact well with your customers, who should also be aligned with your values. When you treat your employees well, they will treat your customers even better.

How to Analyze

To analyze their path to becoming a customer, create a customer journey map. This is the path customers take when considering and purchasing your products. Don't think about this from your company's point of view but from that of the customers. Also, remember that now all your prospects are the same, even though they likely have different personas. For example, if you sell educational products, buyers or influencers might include teachers, principals, or parents.

There are typically three stages in a customer journey map: Awareness, Consideration, and Purchase. For each of these, ask yourself what the prospect or customer is feeling or doing? What are their possible action steps? What and where is the buyer researching? Finally, how will the company move the buyer along toward purchase?

The First Steps

Small business owners are busy—especially now when many are just trying to stay in business. But, unfortunately, so many of their days are reactive without a lot of planning or forethought. You may have a plan to work on strategic actions that can move your company forward, but then the tactical problems of the day get in the way. For example, a specific customer's problem takes precedent over better serving all your customers.

Remember that reviews rule. Customer service is the new marketing. As discussed, reputation is one of the most essential tools in marketing. And customer service is a critical component in building a solid company reputation that keeps people loyal. But what gets and keeps people buying a product has changed. For most of the last century, consumers believed what a company said in its advertisements. This resulted from businesses hiring advertising agencies (as shown in Mad Men) to develop slick slogans delivered by celebrities to influence what products customers would buy.

Today, the internet has allowed society to move from this one-way medium to a more interactive buying process. According to BIA/Kelsey Group, an astounding 97% of customers research products online before buying. But what's even more surprising is the information they seek. Of course, consumers want to know about the latest features, prices, and product availability.

But they also want to know what other consumers think about the products and the company. Today, these reviews have a higher level of credibility than any company-directed advertising and most directly influence what the consumer eventually buys. As previously discussed, 92% of consumers say they trust "earned media" (word of mouth and recommendations from friends), which is far ahead of all other forms of advertising.

This peer-review system is familiar to users of sites like Amazon, eBay, Tripadvisor, or Yelp. Consumers value the "human voice" more than corporate messaging. Plus, Google search engine results about a particular company or product never vanish; they can be found forever.

The immediate electronic delivery of products and fast worldwide shipments of goods make most products commodities since they're available across vast geographies. As a result, price competition has become intense. This presents a considerable challenge for most small business owners because their competitors can now be anywhere in the world. As a result, the only truly sustainable competitive advantage for any small business is its customer service. In fact, according to an American Express survey, 70% of customers are willing to spend more with companies that provide excellent customer service.

Why You Won't Do It Initially

Change when it comes to customers is especially hard since what a great experience means differs from customer to customer and from interaction to interaction. In the end, customers only remember their peak or previous experience with your company. While you can't please all the customers all the time (and the customer is not always right), most small business owners give up on an outstanding customer experience early on, tagging it as unrealistic. But if it was so unrealistic, how were your competitors able to do it?

Take These Next Steps

Try to improve each customer's communication.

B.C. (before computers) business owners sent customers letters, called them on the phone, or visited a customer in person. There were really only these three ways to "talk." As a result, business communication was much more straightforward. Now customers can contact a business through chat, social media, email, voice mail, and fax. With a smartphone in every consumer's hand, there are so many ways to communicate at all times of the day or night. What makes it even more difficult is that customers expect an answer immediately, and many small businesses stink at communicating with their customers. They don't have a unified plan to monitor all communication channels, and they don't get back to customers quickly. You cannot afford to make these mistakes: Customer response time significantly impacts a small business's reputation and sales.

Here's how your company can improve communication:

- Email should be replied to now. Do you know the primary email address customers use when contacting your company? If you don't, figure it out or assign a new one. Then put an immediate auto responder on it, stating how long it will take for someone to get back to the customer—and make darn sure a rep replies within the specified time!

- Only offer chat if you can staff it for an extended period of time. Review your website traffic and find out when most users visit. Be careful if you decide to outsource this function since that company may not have enough information to really help your customers. Do not offer mobile phone chat unless this is the targeted customers' favorite form of communication.

- Depending on the volume of calls, it may not be practical to answer every call live. However, automated answer trees should be limited and only go one level deep before accessing a live person, so have a live person standing by. There is nothing more frustrating than being in "voice mail jail," where a real person is always just out of reach.

- Make all calls "first and final." Whoever "catches" the first message from the customer should track it through to completion (and install a system for this). The biggest complaint most consumers have when they call a company, especially customer service, is repeatedly getting passed off to someone else and having to re-explain their issue.

Consumers are talking online about your business—make sure it's positive. The familiar statistic was that an unhappy customer would tell seven people. Now through social media and online review sites, they can tell millions! Remember when United Airlines broke Dave Carroll's guitar? He produced a video that was seen by seven million people and negatively impacted United's stock price.

Monitor customer reviews.

Boost your customer service—and get great online reviews—by following these four steps:

1—Listen and learn: Sign up for Google Alerts or with a trusted reputation management service to see what people say about your business (and your competitors). Don't be afraid to hear what your customers think. You can track your reputation across the entire web. Read the good and bad comments, so you can be ready to act.

2—Engage constructively: Thank your business's fans and encourage them to spread the word about your company. Also, answer comments from your company's critics by acknowledging the issue and offering a remedy, if appropriate. Remaining silent is not an advantage. When flying, I always get excellent help on the Twitter feed from American Airlines, which employs dozens of people around the clock to monitor it. They use this customer service tool to turn around the perception of an industry that typically does not communicate well.

3—Join the conversation: Be helpful in any area where your business has expertise. Give advice frequently without selling anything. This helps solidify your relationships with customers and prospects, making them more likely to buy from you when they need your service or product.

4—Track it over time: Are your social media efforts leading to more positive comments? Find out where the comments and reviews are coming from so you can focus your attention (and possibly your advertising) on those sites.

Turn customer service into a profit center.

Think about how much money your company makes over the lifetime of a customer. Smart companies invest in this area because it makes them money in the long run. The value of the customer to the company is not just from the initial sale but the follow-on ones as well. Customer service is what keeps customers coming back for more and referring others to your business. A customer's overall economic value can derive from the following:

- Revenue or the time of year the revenue is realized. An order in December when the company is at full capacity may not be as valuable as one in the slower summer months.

- Referrals or positive word of mouth. Having customers act as brand references can build your company exponentially.

- Honest feedback provided to your company to help improve your products or services. This can translate into profits (or save lots of money) in the future.

Enter the new Golden Age of Customer Service.

Take advantage of new technology tools to offer unparalleled personalization and information access to customers. Armed with these tools, small businesses can now project a full-service commitment in the age of self-service. Here are some of the services you will be able to offer.

- **Greet customers by name:** In the past, small business owners knew all their customers by name when they walked into their stores or offices. Today, with web browser cookie technology, if a customer has visited a website before, every company can address their customers by name when they come back to the site. As a result, businesses can even suggest what customers should buy in the future. This "faux personalization" is preferred by customers more than repeatedly visiting a store where the salespeople have no idea who they are.

- **Answer questions 24/7:** In the past, customers would contact a company, then wait weeks for a reply. Today, companies can help customers help themselves through online FAQs, video demos, and chat. Well-designed self-service information on the internet can aid customers any time, day or night, and immediately provide an answer.

- **Offer personalization:** A hundred years ago, a consumer could get a Ford Model T "in any color as long as it was black," according to Henry Ford. Now, most products are customized using technology, allowing customers to create whatever they want. For example, consumers can design their own Nike shoes, mix their own flavors at a Coca-Cola Freestyle machine, or customize a single copy of a book on Amazon.

- **Ship products the same day:** In the old days, to get a product, the customer had to pick it up at the retail location or wait weeks or months for delivery. Today, consumers can not only get a product sent the same day but frequently get it shipped for free! In addition, mega-corporations like Amazon and Walmart also offer same-day delivery to some locations. And, in the printing world, new 3D printing technology enables consumers to "print out" many products themselves.

- **Bring clothes buying to the home or office:** Customers no longer have to travel to a store to try on clothes to get the best fit. Today, there is an app for that! It's a simple as getting the mobile app, then uploading a photo and body specs. The consumer can then choose clothes and see how they fit without leaving their home or office. Need help? Personal online shopping assistants are available to help with the purchase decision.

How to Measure Successful Change

Know your retention rate (how long customers stay with you). After a customer first buys your product or service, how long do they remain your customer? This is an important metric since, as discussed, getting new customers is more expensive than retaining or selling additional services or products to existing ones.

Know the average lifetime value (LTV) of a customer for your company. This is especially important when deciding how many marketing dollars you should invest in getting a new customer. For example, your analysis may show that the average consulting client spends $12,000 with your company over two years. In this case, would you spend $2,000 to get that customer? (The answer is always yes.)

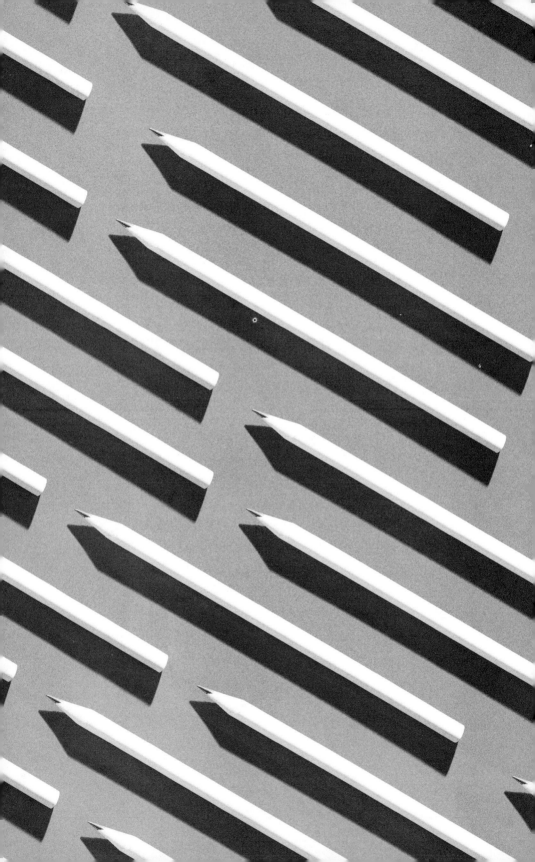

CHAPTER 10

HOW TO CREATE CHANGE IN YOUR PERSONAL AND COMPANY PRODUCTIVITY

What You Do Now

We all have personal systems we've developed over time that help us get things done. For example, my 6th-grade teacher, Mrs. Risley, taught me to take notes by putting a dash before the note, making it an easy-to-read list. I still do this today.

We develop both good and bad productivity habits. But things have got worse today. Strangely, we are at war with ourselves, battling for our own attention.

I keep hearing the same complaints from people:

- "I can't get everything done."
- "There aren't enough hours in the day."
- "I have too many things to do."
- "Multitasking is the only way I can get everything done."

This is all a big lie because being busy is a trap. In fact, according to my speaking coach Victoria Labalme, we compete with one another about how busy we are. "Everyone is busy, but busy-ness has become a cultural symbol of status. People complain about being busy, but the fact is, they're secretly bragging. They even compete over who is busier:

How're you doing?
Good. I'm really busy.
Really? Me, too. I'm sooooo busy.
I'm crazy. I'm totally crazed.
Well, I'm crazy-busy.
Yeah, I'm crazy-busy-nuts."

The big lie is that we don't have enough time. This is an excuse you have repeatedly told yourself to justify not making a change to accomplish what you need to do.

Where to Start to Make the Change

The fact is you do have enough time to get all the important things done to move your business forward. But in reality, you would rather just be busy than be productive; it's easier that way. Being reactive to interruptions or whatever people ask you to do requires very little thinking or planning. Being busy makes you feel more important because you think you have so much to get done. You sacrifice personal time for busywork time. It feels better because you feel guilty when you are not working. Being busy deludes you into thinking you are building a business or making a difference. This is nonsense!

As they say, "You are your own worst enemy"—not the tasks, not the business, not the interruptions, and not the people who work with you. If you make a change and increase you productivity, so will your team.

In fact, you'll discover you actually have plenty of time to think strategically about how you can grow your business and work productively on the tasks to get it there. And you will even have time for your personal life!

I am the most productive person I know. Ask my wife. If I am asked to get something done, it happens.

The one thing most small business owners have in common is that their to-do lists keep getting longer as their days seem to get shorter. This is because, as I said, most people confuse being busy with being productive.

Being busy is just doing stuff at the office; being productive is explicitly working on things that will move your company ahead. To run and grow a profitable business, you need to figure out how to be productive and not just settle for being busy.

Here are actions small business owners can take to be 100% more productive:

- **Choose two tasks:** At the end of every day, take five minutes and make a prioritized list of two things you must accomplish the next day. Do these first before opening up email, checking social media, or tackling anything else on your long to-do list. Then, choose these two items by answering the question, "What two tasks, if I completed them today, would make my day productive?"

- **Turn off notifications:** Stop being reactive. You control the amount of attention you give your electronic devices; don't let them control you with nonstop notifications. Turn off all notifications, and your phone, for set periods of time during the day. Plus, if you work in an office, put up a sign to prevent drop-ins when you don't want to be interrupted.

- **Stop multitasking:** It is a myth that multitasking helps you to get more done. Instead, it allows you to partially complete more tasks poorly. This is because the brain can only focus on a single task well. So, rather than completing two things with average proficiency, do one thing "fantastically" well. Having a split focus makes you less productive. I have a sign on my computer that simply says "FOCUS," which helps me stay on task.

- **Track your time:** The only way to truly know how you are spending your time is to track it. Use time-tracking software, such as Toggl, on your smartphone or desktop to become aware of your work habits, so you can actively change them. When you see how you actually spend your time, you'll be amazed how much of it isn't productive and how often you switch tasks hourly.

- **Hold 15-minute meetings:** Most topics can be addressed in less than 15 minutes. Put all smartphones on the table so no one can look at them. Standing during meetings will always shorten them.

- **Get your inbox to zero:** Most inboxes are a mess. Do a massive inbox cleaning weekly. Delete messages and organize them into separate folders to reach the goal of having zero unread messages in your inbox. Unsubscribe to newsletters you never read. After this massive cleanse is completed, commit to handling every email only once. Once you read an email, reply, delete, file, or set it to follow-up to get it out of your inbox.

- **Create templates:** Most communication is repetitive. Create templates for different types of customers and prospects so you don't have to constantly rewrite the same emails. Using a password manager saves time and increases security.

- **Take a break or get some rest:** Taking a break about every 90 minutes actually makes you more productive. Continuously monitor yourself and your productivity level. Even something as mundane as getting up from your desk to grab a snack can cut that hour-long task in half. Get a good night's sleep. Try the smartphone sleep machine app "Sleep Pillow," which plays sounds that make it easy to fall asleep.

How to Analyze

Don't try to make all the suggestions listed above at once. Trying too many things at one time makes it more likely you will accomplish none of them.

- **Choose two tasks:** Have you done this consistently for two days in a row, and did you tackle those tasks first?

- **Turn off notifications:** Did you turn off notifications for 15 minutes a day? After a week of doing this, can you do it now for 30 minutes?

- **Stop multitasking:** Have you been able to focus on a single task for 15 minutes without getting distracted or doing something else?

- **Track your time:** The night before, did you plan what you would do the next day and how long it would take? Did you then keep track of what you actually did and the time you spent? Did you compare the two? What conclusions did you come to?

- **Hold 15-minute meetings:** How did your first 15-minute meeting go?

- **Get your inbox to zero:** Were you able to get your inbox to zero once this month?

- **Create templates:** What communication templates did you create? Were they helpful?

- **Take a break or get some rest:** For one day this week, did you take at least a five-minute break every 90 minutes?

Why You Won't Do It Initially

One of the biggest challenges we face every day is being accountable for the changes we want to make. We simply don't do the things we say we will. We set out on a daily course that turns into a hamster wheel, and unfortunately, the end of today looks a lot like yesterday.

We start with the best intentions to get the most critical tasks done each day. But somewhere along the way, we get interrupted, delayed, and taken off track by people and things around us. Somehow, we end up doing the same thing over and over again and expect different results.

Does this seem familiar?

- You are overwhelmed by the number of tasks daily you need to do.

- You have difficulty dealing with too many projects to complete at one time.

- You can't prioritize what is most important, so you freeze up.

- You are constantly interrupted.

- Things take longer than you thought to accomplish.

- You would rather do it yourself than delegate to others.

- You are always working, and there seems to be little time for personal activities.

Take These Next Steps Instead

Here are the steps you should take to be more accountable to yourself and accomplish everything you want to do every day.

Step 1: List all your challenges

What are your biggest challenges in each of the following areas, and what prevents you from moving forward or making a change?

- Sales and Marketing
- Leadership and Management
- Finance and Money
- Providing Excellent Customer Experience
- Personal and Team Productivity

What do you think keeps you from moving forward in general when wanting to make a change?

What gets in the way of you being accountable for the things you want to accomplish daily?

Step 2: Pick your challenge and goal

From the list in step 1, pick one challenge you want to focus on and list it here:

What is the goal for overcoming this challenge?

What are the three critical success factors you need to do to accomplish this goal? In other words, what specific things have to happen to achieve that goal.

For each critical success factor, what is the first action you need to take to achieve it?

- Critical success factor 1 action:
- Critical success factor 2 action:
- Critical success factor 3 action:

Step 3: Your to-do list

If you want to be more accountable and get more done, then you need to ruthlessly prioritize your to-do list into these categories. If a task is:

- Urgent and Important: Do it now!
- Urgent and Not Important: Delegate it to someone else.
- Not Urgent and Important: Schedule it to be completed at a convenient time.
- Not Urgent and Not Important: Delete it from your list.

Now take your to-do list and categorize each task with the correct label. Of all the things on your list, what is the most important that needs to get done right now?

How to find a mentor who can support change

It can be lonely at the top. Many small-business owners have told me the one element that's key to their success is finding and working with the right mentor. Many leaders find it challenging to get the unfiltered advice they need while making critical decisions for their companies. A mentor is a person (or group of people) who becomes the trusted outside voice a business owner can rely upon through good times and bad. As I said previously, a mentor is a critical support element for a business owner.

To find the right mentor, every small business owner needs to ask themselves the following questions:

1—Can you admit what you don't know?

This is probably one of the most challenging evaluations for a successful owner to understand. What are your best skills, and where do you need help? Many times, it's hard to figure this out from within the company. Instead, ask former employees and managers for an evaluation (current ones will be too afraid to be honest unless the answers are anonymous). Owners can even take skill evaluation tests like Meyer Briggs to help in this area.

2—How do you best collaborate?

Leaders learn in different ways. Some learn to perform new skills by reading. Others take a visual approach, wanting to see a demonstration of the new skills or a diagram of the process. A business owner needs to find a mentor who can teach the way they most easily learn. This becomes the core of effective collaboration.

3—What qualifications does this person need to have for you to trust them?

Gaining and giving trust is an inexact science. First, you need to understand at what point you freely give your trust to someone. Is it a result of the mentor's experience or your personal interactions with them? Do you trust someone because they were referred to you by a person you already trust? Trust is a vital element of the mentor/mentee relationship. If you don't trust the mentor, you will ignore or marginalize their advice.

4—Will an unpaid or paid mentor work best?

Some leaders believe they will get the most unbiased advice if they don't pay their mentors. They think anyone paid to help them will only give them the information they want to hear. Others believe paid mentors offer the best advice because they're more focused on the issues at hand. There is no one correct answer.

5—Are you a good listener?

One of the hallmarks of a great small business leader is the ability to listen. This doesn't just mean giving the mentor their "say," but understanding how their opinion fits and influences your important decisions.

How to Measure Successful Change

After one month, ask yourself the following questions:

- What was holding you back?
- What are you doing differently that has allowed you to make progress?
- What is still holding you back?
- Where do you still need help?
- How useful was it to set priorities and goals?
- How helpful was the Urgent and Important Matrix?

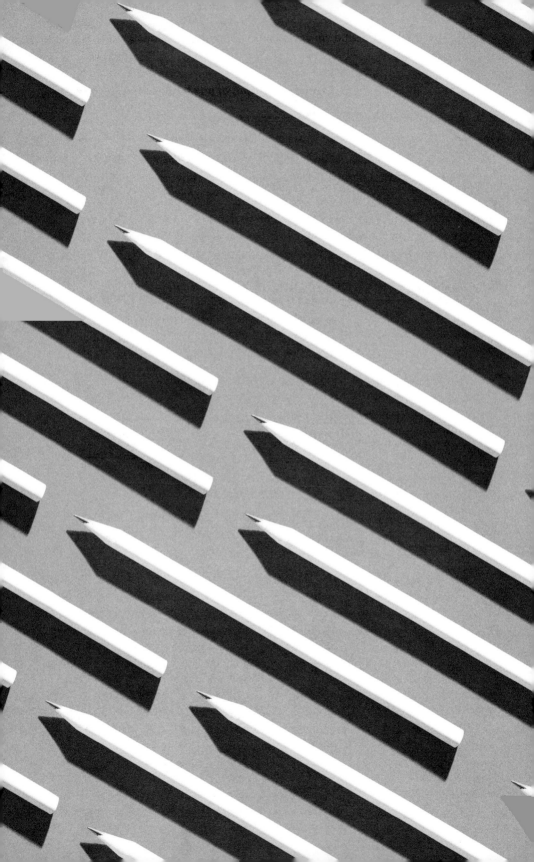

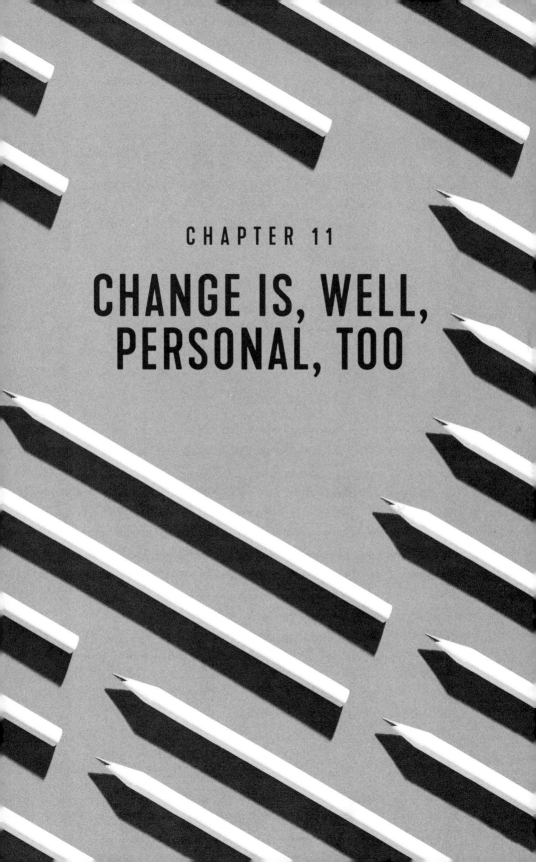

CHAPTER 11

CHANGE IS, WELL, PERSONAL, TOO

What You Do Now

As I got older, I also got stuck in my ways. This is common—it's hard to change our past behaviors. Even if these "ways" haven't been successful or we feel unhappy, our brains encourage us not to make any changes. Our brain reasons that if we change, our past actions must have been wrong—and our brains don't want to accept that we were wrong all this time.

You often hear that "the only constant in life is change." While I dislike this expression, it's true (even as we struggle not to change). The recent COVID-19 pandemic taught us that much. This is a big problem since, ultimately, I believe most of us are uncomfortable with change—or at least science indicates our brains are! But if you are not willing to change, you doom yourself to repeat the same mistakes over and over.

Many times, when I repeatedly do the same thing, I disappoint myself. As Albert Einstein said, "The definition of insanity is doing the same thing over and over again and expecting a different result." Not only can you end up like the Bill Murray character in the movie Groundhog Day, but the monotony it produces just makes you more ineffective.

Sara and I have been married for 30 years. During this time, I've participated in 15 years of personal, group, and marriage therapies. Plus, I have received treatment for medical issues, which I discussed in my previous book, *You Need to Be a Little Crazy; The Truth About Starting and Growing Your Own Business*. I have talked a lot about facing daily interpersonal challenges. These experiences have helped me understand why personal change has been essential for me to move my life forward.

Where to Start to Make the Change

My starkest example happened in 1995. At 35, I was suffering from diabetes, depression, and anxiety. I had stopped eating and lost a third of my body weight. I was one step away from being institutionalized for my emotional issues. If I wanted to stay with my family and get better, I had to change. This started with prescription medication and a lot of talk therapy over the next 18 months.

Despite making progress on these issues, it is still hard for me to change. Luckily, I've found many of the business strategies discussed in Chapter 5 will work in your personal life, as well. The Change Worksheet can help you deal with business and personal issues.

Unfortunately, I've discovered the same issues that held me back personally when I was in my 20's, still do after 40 years:

- Fear of the unknown

- Getting sick or injured
- Not having enough money
- Not being loved or appreciated

While the issues holding me back are the same, 40 years later, I now have better tools to face them and begin to make a change. These fears no longer hold me back from doing most things. Here is where I have started to make changes:

Fear of the unknown and getting sick or injured

About 20 years ago, I suddenly became afraid to fly. Unfortunately, before the global pandemic, my work involved me getting on an airplane every week. This was hard—very hard—for a control freak like me. Turbulence is the worst part of the journey since I have no control over all the bumps and sudden airdrops.

The change I made: To cope, I created a playlist on my iPhone called "Turbulence Tunes" that I listen to when the weather gets rough. It's high-energy music that has me "dancing" in my seat so I can focus on something other than the turbulence, and the "dancing" helps me counteract the other motion that is going on with the airplane. It's a solution that helps me get through to the other side of the turbulence, so I can keep traveling by air.

In addition, in the last 10 years, I've become a germ freak. The Great Pandemic of 2020 certainly heightened my fear of germs (and made me think maybe I was right all along!). But I developed tools that allowed me to go out into the world despite COVID- 19.

The change I made: I bought and used the best N95 masks and plenty of hand sanitizer when I went out into the world. Plus, I exercised and boosted my immune system as best I could. I hired a concierge doctor who I could call at home if I got sick. It didn't make the worry disappear entirely, but it enabled me to change my typical behavior and not feel paralyzed.

Not having enough money

Since I graduated from college way back in 1981, I have been fortunate to earn a good living to support my family. Along the way, I have been fired, unemployed, and gone out of business. I have had lots of money and no money at all. But the fear of not having money goes back to a time when I was a kid. I can remember being awakened at night by my parents arguing about where they'd get the money to pay the bills. While we lived a middle-class lifestyle, my father had been fired and decided to switch to a less lucrative career he enjoyed more. It was an important lesson, but one that, as a kid, was hard to accept when you have to do without.

The change I made: I decided to put some money away for retirement and savings every year and then spend the rest of what I earned on what we needed to live on. Again, this did not take the worry away entirely, but I feel better knowing there's something to fall back on when I'm ready to retire.

Not being loved or appreciated

I am not sure where this fear comes from since, as a child, I felt my parents loved me. At both their funerals, I spoke about how they were great parents and always made us kids the center of their attention.

The change I'm making: I don't feel I've made adequate progress in this area. Later in life, I established a group of friends through cycling, which I regularly reach out to. As we all get older and sometimes more isolated, it is critical to be proactive and reach out to people instead of expecting them to come to us.

How to Analyze It and Take the First Steps

The fear of change should not hold you back from making that change or doing something you may not want to do but needs to get done. My karate training taught me it is okay to be afraid and go ahead and do it anyway.

Yes, I am afraid to fly, and I am a germ freak. But that doesn't prevent me from traveling anywhere globally, even visiting the Dharavi slums in Mumbai, India.

Doing what you are afraid to do does not make the fear go away, but it makes our fears easier to live with. Taking action, despite your fears, is one of the best ways to measure the progress you are making.

Finally, remember we are biologically programmed not to change. So, making a change will always be hard. But work to do it anyway—to improve your business and your life.

AFTERWORD

THE PREVIOUS SECTIONS have offered many suggestions for changes you can make in the specific areas small business owners need help. Do not try to them all at once. Instead, find one that is causing a problem and focus on that small change first. When you have effectively addressed that one, move on to the next.

Being a ChangeMaster is not an all-or-nothing existence. It's not as if once you finally learn how to make the changes you need, you can do that every time. I wish business and life were that simple!

In practice, some days you can be a ChangeMaster and successfully change, while other days, you'd rather avoid making changes and fail. But it's critical to keep practicing the 20 steps discussed in this book to make the changes you know you need to make—slowly and consistently—one at a time.

Practicing may not make perfect, but it does get you closer to your goal than doing nothing.

As I said in my book, *Bounce*: *Failure, Resiliency and the Courage to Achieve Your Next Great Success:*

- Celebrate your success.

- Learn what you can from your setbacks.

- Let go of past successes and setbacks. Then take action that gives you another chance at success.

Change On!

APPENDIX 1

THE CHANGE WORKSHEET

The 20 Steps to Execute a Successful Change

A summary of details from chapter 5.

Note to readers: In order for this exercise to help you, please set aside 20 to 30 minutes to thoughtfully go through the questions. Be very specific and intentional in your answers; don't write in generalities. Do not avoid the tough questions or rush to complete this exercise.

PART 1: BE THE CHANGE

1—What is the change you want to make?

_____

_____

Insight: Be specific and keep it small. To fight your brain's resistance to change, pick something you see as incremental. Remember, big changes are very hard to make all at one time.

Example answer: I want to start reviewing my profit and loss statement every month.

2—How are you currently doing the thing you want to change?

_____

_____

Insight: Do not judge it; just say it.

Example answer: I only review my profit and loss statement when my accountant asks me to.

3—Why do you want to make this change?

_____

_____

Insight: Is this a change thrust upon you by an outside force or generated by something inside the company?

Example answer: I never have enough money to pay all my bills at the end of the month.

4—What will happen if you do not make this change? Be specific.

_____

_____

Insight: Typically, not making necessary changes leads to financial loss or emotional distress.

Example answer: I will not be able to pay my bills, and it keeps me up at night.

5—What inspired you to make this change?

_____

_____

Insight: Your motivation must come from within, not from someone telling you that you need to change. What is that internal motivation (beyond any external forces)?

Example answer: I do not have enough cash to do the things I want in my business.

6—What makes you uncomfortable when you think of making this change?

Insight: We fear change because we fear what will happen if we are successful.

Example answer: I will either become overwhelmed with the financial information presented because I can't understand it or find we are in a worse financial situation than I thought.

7—Who is the one person who can support the change? Why are they the right person for this job?

Insight: This can be a friend or mentor who will keep you accountable but not judge you.

Example answer: My mentor, Rick. He always offers an outside perspective based on his years of success and mentoring others.

8—What precisely can they do to support you in this change? Name a specific action.

Insight: Is this a call or an email check-in? How frequent is it? What action will they be obligated to take?

Example answer: I would like to email him about my progress or challenges once a month so he can help me continue to progress.

9—Reread these tomorrow and make any changes to your answers.

Insight: Repeat this step until you do not make any changes the following day. Even though you want to, do not skip this step!

PART 2: MAKE THE CHANGE

10—What is the smallest step you can take to move toward making this change? Be very specific.

_____

_____

Insight: Think small.

Example answer: Ask my accountant or bookkeeper to review only the sales and net profit from last month and compare it to past results by the 15th of each month.

11—What positive affirmation or reward can you give yourself after you complete the first small step?

_____

_____

Insight: Rewarding yourself for completing this action will help you fight the discomfort of the change. This is a reward for taking action, even if you were not successful.

Example answer: I'd like to treat myself to a bowl of French fries.

12—Share the success or failure of this step with your mentor.

Insight: Do this without judgment. Being too hard on yourself will increase your chances of quitting.

13—After talking with your mentor, rate your success in accomplishing this step from 1 to 5 (lowest to highest). If the rating was not 4 or 5, what could you do better next time?

_____

_____

Insight: Be honest with your progress and rating. You may ask your mentor or support person to rate you as well.

14—How did your success (or failure) reinforce your inspiration to—or your fear of—change?

_____

_____

Insight: This step is not to criticize you but to learn how the results reinforced your inspiration or fears.

15—What is the next smallest step you can take to move toward making this change?

_____

_____

Example answer: Review the major expenses on the profit and loss statement and compare them to past results.

16—What positive affirmation or reward can you give yourself this time after completing this task to fight the discomfort of the change?

_____

_____

Insight: Reap the reward whether you were successful or not. The prize is for taking action on the step.

Example answer: Go for a bicycle ride during work hours.

17—Once again, share the success or failure of this next action or step with your mentor or support person.

Insight: Do this without judgment. Being too hard on yourself will increase your chances of quitting.

18—After talking with your mentor or support person, rate your success in accomplishing this step from 1 to 5 (lowest to highest). If the rating was not 4 or 5, what can you do better next time?

_____

_____

Insight: Be honest with your progress and rating. You may ask your mentor or support person to rate you as well.

19—How did your success (or failure) reinforce your inspiration to—or your fear of—change?

_____

_____

Insight: This step is not to criticize you but to learn how the results reinforced your inspiration or fears.

20—What is the one thing that will help you not give up on making this change?

_____

_____

Insight: Refuse to give up on this change until you have gone through all steps. You may have to do this multiple times. If you consistently fail to complete the steps for this change, try the process again with another change you need to make that will be easier to accomplish.

HOW TO BECOME A CERTIFIED CHANGEMASTER

INALLY, REMEMBER YOU are biologically programmed not to change. So, making a change will always be hard. But work to do it anyway—to improve your business and your life.

Are you interested in helping others make the changes they know they need to make right now? Some of the most satisfying times in my career have been when I was able to get a small business owner unstuck and make the changes that brought them more success and satisfaction.

Work with me to become a Certified ChangeMaster.

This will help you build your own business by training other business owners to accept and make changes based on the practices in this book.

Start your journey today at **www.ChangeMastersBook.com**

RESOURCES

CHAPTER 3: Researching Change: It's Not You, It's the Biology in Your Brain

Section: 1—It's the Basal Ganglia's Fault.

"The Neuroscience of Leadership"
https://www.strategy-business.com/article/06207

"Why It Is So Hard to Change - The Neuroscience Made Simple"
https://drsoph.com/blog/2018/7/6/
why-it-is-so-hard-to-change-the-neuroscience-madesimple

"Why Don't We Forget How to Ride a Bike?"
https://www.scientificamerican.com/article/
why-dont-we-forget-how-to-ride-a-bike/

"The role of the basal ganglia in learning and memory"
https://www.ncbi.nlm.nih.gov/pmc/articles/PMC3772079/

"The Neuroscience of Leadership" https://www.leadershipnow.com/leadingblog/2006/08/the_neuroscience_of_leadership.html

Section 2—Our Expectations Shape Our Reality.

"The Neuroscience of Leadership"
https://www.strategy-business.com/article/06207

"Experience-based brain development: Scientific underpinnings of the importance of early child development in a global world"
https://www.ncbi.nlm.nih.gov/pmc/articles/PMC2528649/

"Changing Mental Maps"
https://robertequinn.com/culture-change/changing-mental-maps/

"Mental Maps and Cognitive Gaps"

https://www.psychologytoday.com/us/blog/shadow-boxing/201601/mental-maps-and-cognitive-gaps

Section 3—The Brain Likes Longevity and Familiarity.

"Longer Is Better"
https://www.sciencedirect.com/science/article/abs/pii/S0022103110001599

"Explained: Why We Don't Like Change"
https://www.huffpost.com/entry/why-we-dont-like-change_b_1072702

Section 4—The Devil Speaks to You.

"Bias in Favor of the Status Quo"
https://www.semanticscholar.org/paper/Bias-in-Favor-of-the-Status-Quo-Eidelman-Crandall/de6e87da1cd40dacb91614cef39331ccdfe362c8

"The Existence Bias"
https://www.ncbi.nlm.nih.gov/pubmed/19857000

Section 5—The Dopamine Rush from Self-Sabotage Instead of Change.

"Why We Self-Sabotage"
https://www.psychologytoday.com/us/blog/unlock-your-true-motivation/201911/why-we-self-sabotage

"6 Reasons Why We Self-Sabotage"
https://www.quickanddirtytips.com/health-fitness/mental-health/6-reasons-why-we-self-sabotage

"No Limits...More Happiness and Success Than You Thought Possible Overcome Your Upper Limits"
https://www.hendricks.com/links/10-6-09_Gay_Article_Experience_Life_Mag.pdf

"Bestselling Author Gay Hendricks Reveals Our Biggest Barriers to Success And How To Overcome Them"
https://www.forbes.com/sites/kathycaprino/2017/08/04/bestselling-author-gay-hendricks-reveals-our-biggest-barriers-to-success-and-how-to-overcome-them/#2bf191bf6222

Section 6—Perfectionism is a Change Problem.

"This Is What the Scary Side of Perfectionism Looks Like" https://www.health.com/condition/depression/bad-perfectionism-signs

"When Perfectionism Becomes a Problem" http://archive.boston.com/news/health/articles/2009/03/02/when_perfectionism_becomes_a_problem/

"Why You Can't Be a Perfectionist and Be an Entrepreneur" https://www.entrepreneur.com/article/310186

"Why Perfectionism Will Kill Your Success as an Entrepreneur" https://wendymaynard.com/entrepreneur-is-perfectionism-holding-you-back-from-the-level-of-success-you-desire/

"The Pros and Cons of Perfectionism, According to Research" https://hbr.org/2018/12/the-pros-and-cons-of-perfectionism-according-to-research

"Is Perfect Good? A meta-analysis of perfectionism in the workplace" https://psycnet.apa.org/buy/2018-27801-001

"'Perfect' employees beware – your perfectionism might be detrimental" https://news.warrington.ufl.edu/faculty-and-research/perfect-employees-beware-your-perfectionism-might-be-detrimental/

"More College Students Seem to Be Majoring in Perfectionism" https://www.nytimes.com/2018/01/18/well/family/more-college-students-seem-to-be-majoring-in-perfectionism.html

"Perfectionism is increasing over time: A meta-analysis of birth cohort differences from 1989 to 2016." https://www.apa.org/news/press/releases/2018/01/perfectionism-young-people

"Perfectionism is increasing over time: A meta-analysis of birth cohort differences from 1989 to 2016." https://psycnet.apa.org/doiLanding?doi=10.1037%2Fbul0000138

"The Tweaker: The Real Genius of Steve Jobs" https://www.newyorker.com/magazine/2011/11/14/the-tweaker

Section 7—Change Based on Incentives and Threats Rarely Succeed Long Term.

"The Neuroscience of Leadership"
https://www.strategy-business.com/article/06207

"Challenging Behaviorist Dogma: Myths About Money and Motivation"
https://www.alfiekohn.org/article/challenging-behaviorist-dogma/

"Managing With the Brain in Mind"
https://www.strategy-business.com/article/09306?gko=9efb2

"When and Why Incentives (Don't) Work to Modify Behavior"
https://rady.ucsd.edu/faculty/directory/gneezy/pub/docs/jep_published.pdf

"Pains and Pleasures of Social Life"
https://www.jstor.org/stable/20403061

Section 8—As You Age, Your Brain Gets Lazy.

"We Know What to Do: Why Don't We Do It"
https://www.mayoclinic.org/we-know-what-to-do-why-dont-we-do-it/art-20454742

"What It Takes to Change Your Brain Patterns After Age 25"
https://www.fastcompany.com/3045424/what-it-takes-to-change-your-brains-patterns-after-age-25

"A Neuroscientist Says We Can Rewire Our Neural Pathways—Here's How"
https://www.mindbodygreen.com/articles/heres-how-we-can-rewire-our-neural-pathways-according-to-a-neurologist

"Neuroscience Hacks to Improve Communication"
https://www.forbes.com/sites/taraswart/2019/01/17/three-neuroscience-insights-to-improve-work-communication/#67a84fbb7f39

"Why Business Is Like the Brain"
https://www.forbes.com/sites/taraswart/2018/07/13/why-business-is-like-the-brain/#bd6e4376c966

"The Truth About How Your Brain Gets Smarter"
https://www.forbes.com/sites/christinecomaford/2014/11/07/the-truth-about-how-your-brain-gets-smarter/#7397ed1c19bc

"Neural activity promotes brain plasticity through myelin growth, study finds"
https://med.stanford.edu/news/all-news/2014/04/neural-activity-promotes-brain-plasticity-through-myelin-growth-study-finds.html

"The Curse of Knowledge: Why Experts Struggle To Explain Their Work"
https://executive.mit.edu/blog/changing-the-mind-of-a-leaderliterally

Section 9—Failure to Track Progress Harms Change.

"'The Ostrich Problem' and The Danger of Not Tracking Your Progress"
https://99u.adobe.com/articles/21387/
the-ostrich-problem-and-the-danger-of-not-tracking-your-progress

"'The Ostrich Problem': Motivated Avoidance or Rejection of Information About Goal Progress"
https://onlinelibrary.wiley.com/doi/full/10.1111/spc3.12071

"Does Monitoring Goal Progress Promote Goal Attainment? A Meta-Analysis of the Experimental Evidence"
https://www.apa.org/pubs/journals/releases/bul-bul0000025.pdf

"Why Do We Buy Insurance: Loss Aversion, Explained"
https://thedecisionlab.com/biases/loss-aversion/

"The Intention–Behavior Gap"
http://eprints.whiterose.ac.uk/107519/3/The%20Intention-Behavior%20Gap%20R1.pdf

"What Is Loss Aversion?""
https://www.scientificamerican.com/article/what-is-loss-aversion/

Section 10—Your Intention is Not the Same as Your Actions.

"Bridging the entrepreneurial intention-behavior gap: The role of commitment and implementation intention"
https://www.researchgate.net/publication/276103351_Bridging_the_
entrepreneurial_intention-behaviour_gap_The_role_of_commitment_and_
implementation_intention

"Does Changing Behavioral Intentions Engender Behavior Change? A Meta-Analysis of the Experimental Evidence"

"Does Monitoring Goal Progress Promote Goal Attainment? A Meta-Analysis of the Experimental Evidence"
https://www.apa.org/pubs/journals/releases/bul-bul0000025.pdf

"The Akrasia Effect: Why We Don't Follow Through on What We Set Out to Do and What to Do About It"
https://jamesclear.com/akrasia

"Why Your Brain Prioritizes Instant Gratification Over Long-Term Goals, According to Science"
https://www.inc.com/melissa-chu/why-your-brain-prioritizes-instant-gratification-o.html

"Study: Brain battles itself over short-term rewards, long-term goals"
https://pr.princeton.edu/news/04/q4/1014-brain.htm

"Self-Determination Theory of Motivation: Why Intrinsic Motivation Matters," https://positivepsychology.com/self-determination-theory/

"Do You Play to Win—or to Not Lose?"
https://hbr.org/2013/03/do-you-play-to-win-or-to-not-lose

"What is Goal Orientation Theory?"
https://implicitbeliefsofintelligencetutorial.weebly.com/performance-vs-learning-goal-orientation.html

"What is Neuroeconomics?"
https://insights.som.yale.edu/insights/what-is-neuroeconomics

"How Motivational Focus Drives Performance"
https://hbr.org/2013/08/how-motivational-focus-drives

"STUDY: Reaching One's Personal Goals: A Motivational Perspective Focused on Autonomy"
https://pdfs.semanticscholar.org/3ae8/0710597cb0f88eeb37f-3c2ad4654f0db1a1d.pdf

"Promotion or Prevention? What's Your Focus and Why It Matters"
https://www.smartliving365.com/promotion-prevention-whats-focus-matters/

"Which Should You Have? Performance Goals Versus Learning Goals"
https://www.leadershipnow.com/leadingblog/2007/12/which_should_you_have_performa.html

"The Intention–Behavior Gap"
http://eprints.whiterose.ac.uk/107519/3/The%20Intention-Behavior%20Gap%20R1.pdf

Chapter 4: One Solution is to Use Science to Train Your Brain for Change

Section 3—For insights to be useful, they need to be generated from within, not given to individuals as conclusions.

"The Neuroscience of Leadership"
https://www.strategy-business.com/article/06207

"A Brain-Based Approach to Coaching"
David Rock, based on an interview with Jeffrey M. Schwartz, M.D.
http://www.crowe-associates.co.uk/wp-content/uploads/2013/10/Coaching-The-Brain-Article1.pdf

"Why Neuroscience Matters to Executives"
https://www.strategy-business.com/article/li00021?gko=01850

"Creative Process: The ARIA Model"
https://www.linkedin.com/pulse/creative-process-aria-model-zsolt-olah/

"'Grow your own brain!' - Self-Directed Neuroplasticity"
https://www.the-cma.org.uk/articles/grow-your-own-brain!-selfdirected-neuroplasticity--6148/

"Self-Directed Neuroplasticity: Consciously Changing Your Brain Function"
https://mentalhealthdaily.com/2015/02/20/self-directed-neuroplasticity-consciously-changing-your-brain-function/

"STUDY: Executive coaching as a transfer of training tool: Effects on productivity in a public agency," https://psycnet.apa.org/record/1997-38390-001
https://search-proquest-com.lib-proxy.fullerton.edu/docview/215943116?accountid=9840&rfr_id=info:xri/sid:primo

Section 4—Agile Brain Pathways for New Habits.

"What it takes to change your brain patterns after age 25"
https://www.fastcompany.com/3045424/what-it-takes-to-change-your-brains-patterns-after-age-25

"A Neuroscientist Says We Can Rewire Our Neural Pathways -- Here's How"
https://www.mindbodygreen.com/articles/
heres-how-we-can-rewire-our-neural-pathways-according-to-a-neurologist

"The Curse Of Knowledge: Why Experts Struggle To Explain Their Work"
https://executive.mit.edu/blog/changing-the-mind-of-a-leaderliterally

Section 5—Take it Easy.

"STUDY: The Intention–Behavior Gap"
http://eprints.whiterose.ac.uk/107519/3/The%20Intention-Behavior%20
Gap%20R1.pdf

"STUDY: Predicting Behaviour from Perceived Behavioural Control
(Sheeran, Trafimow, Armitage)"
British Journal of Social Psychology (2003)

"STUDY: Achievement Goals, Task Performance, and Interest: Why
Perceived Goal Difficulty Matters" (Corwin Senko & Judith M. Harackiewicz)
http://psp.sage.pub.com/content/31/12/1739